Dear Richard
– a taste of Iran –
with love from
Margot + Alan

June 2014

In The Name of God

آربری، آرتورجان، ۱۹۰۵ـ ۱۹۶۹م، گردآورنده
Arberry, Arthur John (پرشین پوئمز)
Persian, poems / editor by A. J. Arberry;
Tehran: Yassavoli, 2005 = 1384
ISBN 978-964-306-302-3 ۲۸۸ص.
فهرستنویسی براساس اطلاعات فیپا.
واژه‌نامه. نمایه. چاپ سوم: ۱۳۹۱
۱. شعر فارسی -- ترجمه شده به انگلیسی -- مجموعه‌ها. الف. عنوان: Persian poems.
PIR۴۰۴۹ / ۸آ۴ الف ۸فا۱/۰۰۸ ۱۳۸۴
کتابخانه ملی ایران ۱۳۷۸۵-۸۳م

چاپ سوم: ۱۳۹۱، چاپ پدیدرنگ، تیراژ: ۳۰۰۰ نسخه

In this book pictures have been adopted from the archive of the General Department of Bonyad Museums.

Persian Poems

Edited by A. J. Arberry
Bazaarcheh Ketab, Enqelab Ave., 13146, Tehran, Iran.
Tel.: (9821) 66461003 Fax: (9821) 66411913
78, Karim Khan Ave., Tehran, Iran.
Tel.: (9821) 88300415 Fax: (9821) 88832038
info@yassavoli.com
www.yassavoli.com
ISBN: 978-964-306-302-3

Persian Poems

AN ANTHOLOGY OF VERSE TRANSLATIONS

EDITED BY

A.J. ARBERY

YASSAVOLI PUBLICATIONS

PREFACE

IN 1772 William Jones, a promising candidate for the Bar, newly elected Fellow of the Royal Society, published a slim volume of *Poems, consisting chiefly of Translations from the Asiatick Languages*. This little book, favourably though not rapturously received at the time, is a landmark in the interpretation of Persian literature, containing as it does the first English verse translation of a Persian poem. A *Persian Song*, which is included in the *Oxford Book of Eighteenth-Century Verse*, appears to us now as a good typical product of its time, a very polished and elegant paraphrase of a famous lyric by Hafez. Its influence, both immediate and subsequent, has been prodigious; the point could be discussed at length, but it will suffice to quote a remark of the late Professor R. M. Hewitt: 'Perhaps we may add to Jones's titles to fame: genuit FitzGerald.'

Jones later went out to India, to be judge in the High Court of Calcutta. There he found many servants of the East India Company fluent in Persian; Warren Hastings himself was a passionate and discriminating collector of Persian manuscripts. To translate Persian poetry into English verse was a fashionable and admired exercise, and Hafez became as much a household name as Horace. This was the age of Joseph Champion, John Richardson, John Nott, John Haddon Hindley; it was the age of Goethe and the *West-oestlicher Diwan,* and Goethe paid handsome tribute to Jones's greatness and the immortal poetry of Hafez. By the time Persian ceased to be the *official* language of literature and administration in British India, the fame of Persian poetry had become so widespread in Europe as to be beyond danger of eclipse. Matthew Arnold, who was not aware of James Atkinson's labours on Ferdowsi but drew his inspiration from a French version, in 1853 introduced *Sohrab and Rostam* to the British public. Six years later came the first edition of Edward FitzGerald's *Ruba'iyat of Omar Khayyam.* Roses and bulbuls spattered the scented pages of mid-Victorian literature. The Persian fashion, stimulated further by the much-publicized state visit of Naser-od Din Shah, reached new heights of popularity. More and more Persian poetry was done into English verse by more and more translators. So, through the fluctuations of taste and interest down the succeeding decades, matters have continued to the present day.

The poetry under discussion has been written over a period of a thousand years, for Persian as a literary language needed some three centuries of gestation following the Arab conquest and the destruction of the Sassanian empire; the parallel instance of English as distinct from Anglo-Saxon has often been cited, and is remarkably close. Ode and lyric seem to have been the first forms to emerge, originally under strong Arabic influence; prosody, rhyming system, and conventional imagery were all largely borrowed from the victors' literature. But at a very early date some unknown genius invented the quatrain, which was presently to be used so brilliantly by Omar Khayyam; this brief epigram clothes a single thought, and each *ruba'i* is an independent creation: it was left to FitzGerald to thread a sequence together to effect the illusion of continuous composition. The ode and the lyric had been monorhymes; Ferdowsi, emulating his less skilful and less persevering predecessor Daqiqi, took over the rhyming couplet, which the Arabs had known but neglected, and made it the basis of the Persian epic. He is also credited —though the attribution is now disputed— with having written the first idyll, a brief epopee on the story of Joseph and Potiphar's wife; it fell to Nezami to perfect this form, which many others afterwards practised. Didactic writing seems to have been endemic in Persia, the homeland of saws and proverbs; Naser Khosrow preached by ode, Sana'i and Rumi in couplets, but the supreme master of popular philosophy was Sa'di, his fellow townsman Hafez being the acknowledged king of lyric. With the death of Jami, Persian poetry fell into a rapid decline; though still composed abundantly, not only in Persia but also in the neighbouring lands of Turkey and India, it lost its creative power and specialized more and more in clever or vapid imitation. The impact of European culture towards the end of the last century has now set up a new ferment in the Persian mind, and originality has once more returned to revitalize the tradition of Ferdowsi, Sa'di, Hafez, and Jami.

Persian poetical literature is of immense bulk, and the greater, albeit the inferior, part of it still remains unpublished. It is one of the abiding glories of British rule in India that it was during the days of the East India Company, and through the enthusiasm and skill of British scholar-administrators, that the first impressive beginnings were made in reducing the classical poetry of Persia to print. The first edition of Hafez was published by Upjohn's Calcutta Press in 1791. The collected works of Sa'di were printed in two folio volumes at Calcutta between 1791 and 1795; J. H. Harington presided over the enterprise, the Honourable Company's Press executed the great commission. Matthew Lumsden brought out in 1811, at the same address, a large volume containing one-eighth of Ferdowsi's *Shahnameh;* the entire epic was produced at the Baptist Mission Press eighteen years later by Turner Macan. Let the memory of those glorious pioneers never be forgotten; the books they printed provided the translators with more or less reliable texts to work upon, and inspired subsequent scholars all over the world to emulate their example. Thus it was a British scholar, R. A. Nicholson, who in our times laboured unremittingly to produce the first critical edition of Rumi's *Masnavi,* the greatest mystical poem ever written.

How should Persian poetry be translated? Sir William Jones elected to use rhyming verse; his choice, obviously influenced by the tradition of his century, has been generally applauded and followed by his successors. In A *Persian Song* he paraphrased, though not so freely as did FitzGerald in his *Ruba'iyat.* It is not much remembered that he made a version of a poem by Jami, in which he contrived to imitate, not unsuccessfully, the monorhyme which is so characteristic a feature of the Persian lyric; anticipating by more than a century the ponderous experiments of Walter Leaf and John Payne. No one who has struggled through the latter's three-volume translation of Hafez will survive the ordeal still open to persuasion that that is the right way to translate Persian poetry. Hafez indeed provides the acid test: he is a writer of the utmost charm and delicacy, and any version which makes him unreadable or ridiculous is obviously on wrong lines. Rhymed translation is always something of an acrobatic performance: translation in monoryhme might be likened to setting an elephant to cross a tightrope.

For nearly two centuries now metre, and usually rhyme, have been thought indispensable to any respectable version of Persian poetry. All the examples collected in this volume are in metre; most are also rhymed. So far no successful translation into the modern unrhymed and rhythmic cadences has been published; therefore none is quoted, though this does not mean that the editor is convinced that no such renderings will ever succeed. That is for the future to say; meanwhile we can only pass judgment upon what lies to hand. Any volume of verse translations is bound to compare unfavourably with an equal amount of original writing, provided the latter is not wholly inferior; it is doubtful, however, whether any volume of verse translation from or into any language starts with the advantage of a piece so famous and memorable as FitzGerald's *Ruba'iyat:* if nothing else had been done, that poem is sufficient witness to the quality of Persian poetry. Readers of this book will form their own opinions as to whether there is anything else that stands near, or not too distant; the editor, whose verdict is biased because he has himself entered the lists, claims for consideration at any rate FitzGerald's other versions, the *Bird-Parliament* and *Salaman and Absal;* to which he would add the work of Sir William Jones, James Atkinson, Gertrude Bell, Reynold Nicholson, and some pieces of Edward Granville Browne, Edward Palmer, Walter Leaf, and Richard Le Gallienne. Other translators, some of whom have been excluded altogether for one or another adequate reason, have done good work at times; and the general level of achievement is surely not contemptible.

There is an art of translation, and there is an art of reading translations. About the former much has been written, and opinions have varied widely; to quote two titles out of an extensive literature, J. B. Postgate's *Translation and Translations* (Bell, 1922) and E. G. Bates's *Modern Translation* (O.U.P., 1936) supply plentiful food for thought. Less has been said on how to read what others have striven to translate; yet the reader also needs to prepare himself for his task, if he is to derive from the exercise the advantage he looks hopefully to gain. First, he must not expect to be equal to a lively appreciation of all that he reads, unless he learns something of the nature of the language and literature from which the translations have been made. Even FitzGerald will mean more to him if he understands the references, and is aware of the background to Omar Khayyam's poems; if he will not be content to flounder indolently in the warm waters of imperfectly apprehended but comfortable words. There is much in Persian poetry which is readily acceptable: the rapid narrative of Ferdowsi, the sententious moralizing of Sa'di, the Bacchanalian logic of Omar Khayyam, touch immediately responsive chords. But there is far more in Persian poetry which escapes notice altogether and is therefore in danger of falling flat, unless the reader is aware of what the poet is trying to do and say, within the framework of his own literary conventions.

Secondly, the reader of translations, like the reader of poetry in general, should not be over-gluttonous, or he will quickly satiate his appetite, and find himself suffering from acute aesthetic indigestion. Should such a misfortune befall him, he will no doubt be apt to condemn the fare that has lain before him: more probably it is himself who is to blame. Translations are to be sampled and savoured, not to be wolfed; the palate, pleasantly stimulated by the unaccustomed dishes, will develop painlessly a new sensitivity; and so little by little the spread banquet will be consumed, leaving behind a fragrant memory and a delightfully enlarged experience.

ACKNOWLEDGMENTS

THE editor has endeavoured to be exact in reproducing the texts as approved for print by the translators themselves; he has, however, in some instances modified the spelling and punctuation to conform with modern practice. In one instance, Joseph Champion's versions of Ferdowsi, he had the advantage of access in Cambridge University Library to a copy which had been corrected after publication by the translator. Where translators have used diacritical points in transliterating Persian names, these have been omitted because they are liable to irritate the non-specialist reader and add nothing to the understanding of the original. Of FitzGerald's *Ruba'iyat* the texts of the first and fourth editions have been given, so as to illustrate the changes made by the translator over the years. These two texts have been carefully checked against the originals, in the hope of excluding the inaccuracies which disfigured most if not all previous reprints; even probable misprints, such as \`lightning' in Stanza XIV of the first edition (fourth edition: \`lighting'), have been faithfully copied.

For permission to include copyright material thanks are hereby expressed to George Allen & Unwin Ltd for extracts from Rumi, translated by R. A. Nicholson; to the Cambridge University Press for translations by E. G. Browne from *A Literary History of Persia,* and translations by R. A. Nicholson from *Eastern Poetry and Prose;* to William Heinemann Ltd for translations by Gertrude Bell from *Poems from the Divan of Hafiz;* to Mrs A. V. Williams Jackson for an extract from *Early Persian Poetry,* translated by the late Professor A. V. Williams Jackson; to Luzac & Co. Ltd for translations by A. J. Arberry from *Immortal Rose;* to John Murray Ltd for translations by A. J. Arberry from *Mysteries of Selflessness;* to L. C. Page & Co. for extracts from Richard Le Gallienne's translation of *Odes from the Divan of Hafiz;* to the Richards Press Ltd for translations by the late Walter Leaf from *Versions of Hafiz;* and to Emery Walker Ltd for extracts from A. J. Arberry's translation of *Ruba'iyat of Rumi.*

A. J. A.

ACKNOWLEDGMENTS

[illegible]

SELECT BIBLIOGRAPHY

THE WORKS IN GENERAL. A. J. Arberry: *British Contributions to Persian Studies*, London, Longmans, 1942; *Immortal Rose, an Anthology of Persian Lyrics*, London, Luzac, 1948; E. G. Browne: *A Literary History of Persia*, 4 vols., Cambridge, 1928; A. V. Williams Jackson: *Early Persian Poetry*, New York, Macmillan, 1920; W. Jones: *Works, 13 vols.*, London, 1807; R. A. Nicholson: *Translations of Eastern Poetry and Prose*, Cambridge, 1922; E. H. Palmer: *The Song of the Reed and Other Poems*, London, Trübner, 1877.

INDIVIDUAL POETS. ATTAR: see Jami. FERDOWSI: *The Poems of Ferdosi*, translated by J. Champion, Calcutta, 1785; *The Shah Nameh of the Persian Poet Firdausi*, translated and abridged in prose and verse by J. Atkinson, London, Warne, 1886.

HAFEZ: *A Specimen of Persian Poetry; or, Odes of Hafez*, by J. Richardson, London, 1774; *Select Odes from the Persian Poet Hafez*, translated into English verse by J. Nott, London, 1787; *Persian Lyrics; or, scattered Poems from the Diwan-i Hafez*, by J. H. Hindley, London, 1800; *Poems from the Divan of Hafiz*, by G. L. Bell, London, Heinemann, 1897; *Versions from Hafiz*, an essay in Persian metre, by W. Leaf, London, Grant Richards, 1898; *The Poems of Shemseddin Mohammed Hafiz of Shiraz*, by J. Payne, London, Villon Society, 1901; *Odes from the Divan of Hafiz*, freely rendered from literal translations, by R. Le Gallienne, Boston, Page, 1905; *Fifty Poems of Hafiz*, by A. J. Arberry, Cambridge, 1947.

EQBAL: *The Mysteries of Selflessness*, translated into English verse by A. J. Arberry, London, Murray, 1953.

IRAQI: *The Song of Lovers*, translated into English verse by A. J. Arberry, Bombay, Oxford University Press, 1939.

JAMI: *Salaman and Absal*, an allegory translated from the Persian of Jami; together with a bird's-eye view of Farid-od Din Attar's *Bird-Parliament*, by E. FitzGerald, Boston, Page, 1899.

NEZAMI: *Laili and Majnun*, a poem, from the original Persian of Nazami, by J. Atkinson, London, 1836.

OMAR KHAYYAM: *Ruba'iyat of Omar Khayyam, the Astronomer-poet of Persia*, translated into English verse [by E. FitzGerald], London, Quaritch, 1859; *Ruba'iyat of Omar Khayyam; and the Salaman and Absal of Jami*. Rendered into English verse [by E. FitzGerald, London, Quaritch, 1879; *Ruba'iyat* of *Omar Khayyam*, a variorum edition of Edward FitzGerald's renderings into English verse, edited by F. H. Evans, London, privately printed, 1904.

RUMI: *The Mesnevi ... of Mevlana (Our Lord) Jelalu-'d-Din, Muhammed, er-Rumi*, book the first, translated and the poetry versified, by J. W. Redhouse, London, Trübner, 1881; *The Ruba'iyat of Jalal al-Din Rumi*, select translations into English verse, by A. J. Arberry, London, Emery Walker, 1949; *Rumi, Poet and Mystic*, selections translated by R. A. Nicholson, London, Allen & Unwin, 1950.

SA'DI: *Flowers of the East*, with an introductory sketch of Oriental Poetry and Music, by E. Pocock, London, 1833; A *Few Flowers from the Garden of Sheikh Saadi Shirazi*, by W. W. Mackinnon, Calcutta, 1877; *The Gulistan; or, Rose-Garden of ... Sadi*, by E. B. Eastwick, London, Trübner, 1880; *The Garden of Fragrance*, by G. S. Davie, London, Kegan Paul, 1882; *The Gulistan; being the Rose-Garden of Shaikh Sa'di*, the first four Babs ... translated in prose and verse by Sir E. Arnold, London, Burleigh, 1899.

CONTENTS

QUATRAIN

OMAR KHAYYAM

Edward FitzGerald
First Edition, 1859

I

Awake! for Morning in the Bowl of Night
Has flung the Stone that puts the Stars to Flight:
    And Lo! the Hunter of the East has caught
The Sultan's Turret in a Noose of Light.

II

Dreaming when Dawn's Left Hand was in the Sky
I heard a Voice within the Tavern cry:
    'Awake, my Little ones, and fill the Cup
Before Life's Liquor in its Cup be dry.'

III

And, as the Cock crew, those who stood before
The Tavern shouted: 'Open then the Door!
    You know how little while we have to stay,
And, once departed, may return no more.'

IV

Now the New Year reviving old Desires,
The thoughtful Soul to Solitude retires,
    Where the WHITE HAND OF MOSES on the Bough
Puts out, and Jesus from the Ground suspires.

V

Eram indeed is gone with all its Rose,
And Jamshid's Sev'n-ring'd Cup where no one knows;
    But still the Vine her ancient Ruby yields,
And still a Garden by the Water blows.

VI

And David's Lips are lock't; but in divine
High-piping Pahlavi, with 'Wine! Wine! Wine!
Red Wine!' – the Nightingale cries to the Rose,
That yellow Cheek of her's to'incarnadine.

VII

Come, fill the Cup, and in the Fire of Spring
The Winter Garment of Repentance fling:
The Bird of Time has but a little way
To fly—and Lo! the Bird is on the Wing.

VIII

And look—a thousand Blossoms with the Day
Woke—and a thousand scatter'd into Clay:
And this first Summer Month that brings the Rose
Shall take Jamshid and Kaiqobad away.

IX

But come with old Khayyam, and leave the Lot
Of Kaiqobad and Kaikhosrow forgot:
Let Rostam lay about him as he will,
Or Hatam Ta'i cry Supper—heed them not.

X

With me along some Strip of Herbage strown
That just divides the desert from the sown,
Where name of Slave and Sultan scarce is known,
And pity Sultan Mahmoud on his Throne.

XI

Here with a Loaf of Bread beneath the Bough,
A Flask of Wine, a Book of Verse—and Thou
Beside me singing in the Wilderness—
And Wilderness is Paradise enow.

XII

'How sweet is mortal Sovranty!' –think some:
Others: 'How blest the Paradise to come!'
   Ah, take the Cash in hand and waive the Rest;
Oh, the brave Music of a *distant* Drum!

XIII

Look to the Rose that blows about us –Lo,
Laughing,' she says, 'into the World I blow:
   And at once the silken Tassel of my Purse
Tear, and its Treasure on the Garden throw.'

XIV

The Worldly Hope men set their Hearts upon
Turns Ashes –or it prospers; and anon,
   Like Snow upon the Desert's dusty Face
Lighting a little hour or two –is gone.

XV

And those who husbanded the Golden Grain,
And those who flung it to the Winds like Rain,
   Alike to no such aureate Earth are turn'd
As, buried once, Men want dug up again.

XVI

Think, in this batter'd Caravanserai
Whose Doorways are alternate Night and Day,
   How Sultan after Sultan with his Pomp
Abode his Hour or two, and went his way.

XVII

They say the Lion and the Lizard keep
The Courts where Jamshid gloried and drank deep:
   And Bahram, that great Hunter –the Wild Ass
Stamps o'er his Head, and he lies fast asleep.

XVIII

I sometimes think that never blows so red
The Rose as where some buried Caesar bled;
That every Hyacinth the Garden wears
Dropt in its Lap from some once lovely Head.

XIX

And this delightful Herb whose tender Green
Fledges the River's Lip on which we lean –
Ah, lean upon it lightly! for who knows
From what once lovely Lip it springs unseen!

XX

Ah, my Belovéd, fill the Cup that clears
TO-DAY of past Regrets and future Fears –
To-morrow? –Why, To-morrow I may be
Myself with Yesterday's Sev'n Thousand Years.

XXI

Lo! some we loved, the loveliest and best
That Time and Fate of all their Vintage prest,
Have drunk their Cup a Round or two before,
And one by one crept silently to Rest.

XXII

And we, that now make merry in the Room
They left, and Summer dresses in new Bloom,
Ourselves must we beneath the Couch of Earth
Descend, ourselves to make a Couch –for whom?

XXIII

Ah, make the most of what we yet may spend,
Before we too into the Dust descend:
Dust into Dust, and under Dust, to lie,
Sans Wine, sans Song, sans Singer, and –sans End!

XXIV

Alike for those who for *TO-DAY* prepare,
And those that after a *TO-MORROW* stare,
A Muezzin from the Tower of Darkness cries:
'Fools! your Reward is neither Here nor There!'

XXV

Why, all the Saints and Sages who discuss'd
Of the Two Worlds so learnedly, are thrust
Like foolish Prophets forth; their Words to Scorn
Are scatter'd, and their Mouths are stopt with Dust.

XXVI

Oh, come with old Khayyam, and leave the Wise
To talk: one thing is certain, that Life flies;
One thing is certain, and the Rest is Lies:
The Flower that once has blown for ever dies.

XXVII

Myself when young did eagerly frequent
Doctor and Saint, and heard great Argument
About it and about: but evermore
Came out by the same Door as in I went.

XXVIII

With them the Seed of Wisdom I did sow,
And with my own hand labour'd it to grow:
And this was all the Harvest that I reap'd:
'I came like Water, and like Wind I go.'

XXIX

Into this Universe, and *why* not knowing,
Nor *whence*, like Water willy-nilly flowing:
And out of it, as Wind along the Waste,
I know not *whither*, willy-nilly blowing.

XXX

What, without asking, hither hurried *whence*?
And, without asking, *whither* hurried hence!
Another and another Cup to drown
The Memory of this Impertinence!

XXXI

Up from Earth's Centre through the Seventh Gate
I rose, and on the Throne of Saturn sate,
And many Knots unravel'd by the Road;
But not the Knot of Human Death and Fate.

XXXII

There was a Door to which I found no Key;
There was a Veil past which I could not see:
Some little Talk awhile of ME and THEE
There seemed —and then no more of THEE and ME.

XXXIII

Then to the rolling Heav'n itself I cried,
Asking: 'What Lamp had Destiny to guide
Her little Children stumbling in the Dark?'
And—'A blind Understanding!' Heav'n replied.

XXXIV

Then to this earthen Bowl did I adjourn,
My Lip the secret Well of Life to learn:
And Lip to Lip it murmur'd: 'While you live
Drink! —for once dead you never shall return.'

XXXV

I think the Vessel, that with fugitive
Articulation answer'd, once did live,
And merry-make; and the cold Lip I kiss'd,
How many Kisses might it take—and give!

Mas'oud Honarkar, Safavid school, 21×14 cm., 2001

Mas'oud Honarkar,

l, 19×25 cm., 2000

Mas'oud Honarkar, Safavid school, 29×38 cm., 2000

XXXVI

For in the Market-place, one Dusk of Day,
I watch'd the Potter thumping his wet Clay:
And with its all-obliterated Tongue
It murmur'd: 'Gently, Brother, gently, pray!'

XXXVII

Ah, fill the Cup—what boots it to repeat
How Time is slipping underneath our Feet:
Unborn TO-MORROW, and dead YESTERDAY,
Why fret about them if TO-DAY be sweet!

XXXVIII

One Moment in Annihilation's Waste,
One Moment, of the Well of Life to taste—
The Stars are setting and the Caravan
Starts for the Dawn of Nothing—Oh, make haste!

XXXIX

How long, how long, in infinite Pursuit
Of This and That endeavour and dispute?
Better be merry with the fruitful Grape
Than sadden after none, or bitter, Fruit.

XL

You know, my Friends, how long since in my House
For a new Marriage I did make Carouse:
Divorced old barren Reason from my Bed,
And took the Daughter of the Vine to Spouse.

XLI

For 'IS' and ' IS-NOT' though *with* Rule and Line,
And 'UP-AND-DOWN' *without*, I could define,
I yet in all I only cared to know
Was never deep in anything but—Wine.

XLII

And lately, by the Tavern Door agape,
Came stealing through the Dusk an Angel Shape
   Bearing a Vessel on his Shoulder; and
He bid me taste of it; and 'twas —the Grape!

XLIII

The Grape that can with Logic absolute
The Two-and-Seventy jarring Sects confute:
   The subtle Alchemist that in a Trice
Life's leaden Metal into Gold transmute.

XLIV

The mighty Mahmoud, the victorious Lord,
That all the misbelieving and black Horde
   Of Fears and Sorrows that infest the Soul
Scatters and slays with his enchanted Sword.

XLV

But leave the Wise to wrangle, and with me
The Quarrel of the Universe let be:
   And, in some corner of the Hubbub coucht,
Make Game of that which makes as much of Thee.

XLVI

For in and out, above, about, below,
'Tis nothing but a Magic Shadow-show,
   Play'd in a Box whose Candle is the Sun,
Round which we Phantom Figures come and go.

XLVII

And if the Wine you drink, the Lip you press,
End in the Nothing all Things end in—Yes—
   Then fancy while Thou art, Thou art but what
Thou shalt be—Nothing—Thou shalt not be less.

XLVIII

While the Rose blows along the River Brink,
With old Khayyam the Ruby Vintage drink:
   And when the Angel with his darker Draught
Draws up to Thee —take that, and do not shrink.

XLIX

'Tis all a Chequer-board of Nights and Days
Where Destiny with Men for Pieces plays:
   Hither and thither moves, and mates, and slays,
And one by one back in the Closet lays.

L

The Ball no Question makes of Ayes and Noes,
But Right or Left as strikes the Player goes;
   And He that toss'd Thee down into the Field,
He knows about it all—HE knows—HE knows!

LI

The Moving Finger writes; and, having writ,
Moves on: nor all thy Piety nor Wit
   Shall lure it back to cancel half a Line
Nor all thy Tears wash out a Word of it.

LII

And that inverted Bowl we call The Sky,
Whereunder crawling coop't we live and die,
   Lift not thy hands to *It* for help —for It
Rolls impotently on as Thou or I.

LIII

With Earth's first Clay They did the Last Man's knead,
And then of the Last Harvest sow'd the Seed:
   Yea, the first Morning of Creation wrote
What the Last Dawn of Reckoning shall read.

LIV

I tell Thee this—When, starting from the Goal,
Over the shoulders of the flaming Foal
    Of Heav'n Parwin and Mushtari they flung,
In my predestin'd Plot of Dust and Soul

LV

The Vine had struck a Fibre; which about
If clings my Being—let the Sufi flout;
    Of my Base Metal may be filed a Key,
That shall unlock the Door he howls without.

LVI

And this I know: whether the one True Light
Kindle to Love, or Wrath-consume me quite,
    One Glimpse of It within the Tavern caught
Better than in the Temple lost outright.

LVII

O Thou, who didst with Pitfall and with Gin
Beset the Road I was to wander in,
    Thou wilt not with Predestination round
Enmesh me, and impute my Fall to Sin?

LVIII

O Thou, who Man of baser Earth didst make,
And who with Eden didst devise the Snake;
    For all the Sin wherewith the Face of Man
Is blacken'd, Man's Forgiveness give —and take!

KÚZA-NÁMA

LIX

Listen again. One Evening at the Close
Of Ramazan, ere the better Moon arose,
  In that old Potter's Shop I stood alone
With the clay Population round in Rows.

LX

And, strange to tell, among that Earthen Lot
Some could articulate, while others not:
  And suddenly one more impatient cried:
'Who *is* the Potter, pray, and who the Pot?'

LXI

Then said another: 'Surely not in vain
My Substance from the common Earth was ta'en,
  That He who subtly wrought me into Shape
Should stamp me back to common Earth again.'

LXII

Another said: 'Why, ne'er a peevish Boy
Would break the Bowl from which he drank in Joy;
  Shall He that *made* the Vessel in pure Love
And Fansy, in an after Rage destroy!'

LXIII

None answer'd this; but after Silence spake
A Vessel of a more ungainly Make:
  'They sneer at me for leaning all awry;
What! did the Hand then of the Potter shake?'

LXIV

Said one: 'Folks of a surly Tapster tell,
And daub his Visage with the Smoke of Hell;
  They talk of some strict Testing of us—Pish!
He's a Good Fellow, and 'twill all be well.'

LXV

Then said another with a long-drawn Sigh:
'My Clay with long oblivion is gone dry:
But fill me with the old familiar Juice,
Methinks I might recover by-and-bye!'

LXVI

So while the Vessels one by one were speaking,
One spied the little Crescent all were seeking:
And then they jogg'd each other: 'Brother! Brother!
Hark to the Porter's Shoulder-knot a-creaking!'

LXVII

Ah, with the Grape my fading Life provide,
And wash my Body whence the Life has died,
And in a Winding-sheet of Vine-leaf wrapt,
So bury me by some sweet Garden-side.

LXVIII

That ev'n my buried Ashes such a Snare
Of Perfume shall fling up into the Air,
As not a True Believer passing by
But shall be overtaken unaware.

LXIX

Indeed the Idols I have loved so long
Have done my Credit in Men's Eye much wrong:
Have drown'd my Honour in a shallow Cup,
And sold my Reputation for a Song.

LXX

Indeed, indeed, Repentance oft before
I swore—but was I sober when I swore?
And then and then came Spring, and Rose-in-hand
My threadbare Penitence apieces tore.

LXX

And much as Wine has play'd the Infidel,
And robb'd me of my Robe of Honour —well,
I often wonder what the Vintners buy
One half so precious as the Goods they sell.

LXXII

Alas, that Spring should vanish with the Rose!
That Youth's sweet-scented Manuscript should close!
The Nightingale that in the Branches sang,
Ah whence, and whither flown again, who knows!

LXXIII

Ah Love! could thou and I with Fate conspire
To grasp this sorry Scheme of Things entire,
Would not we shatter it to bits —and then
Remould it nearer to the Heart's Desire!

LXXIV

Ah Moon of my Delight who know'st no wane,
The Moon of Heav'n is rising once again:
How oft hereafter rising shall she look
Through this same Garden after me —in vain!

LXXV

And when Thyself with shining Foot shall pass
Among the Guests Star-scatter'd on the Grass,
And in thy joyous Errand reach the Spot
Where I made one —turn down an empty Glass!

Fourth Edition, 1879

I

Wake! For the Sun who scatter'd into flight
The Stars before him from the Field of Night,
  Drives Night along with them from Heav'n, and strikes
The Sultan's Turret with a Shaft of Light.

II

Before the phantom of False morning died,
Methought a Voice within the Tavern cried:
  'When all the Temple is prepared within,
Why nods the drowsy Worshipper outside?'

III

And, as the Cock crew, those who stood before
The Tavern shouted: 'Open then the Door!
  You know how little while we have to stay,
And, once departed, may return no more.'

IV

Now the New Year reviving old Desires,
The thoughtful Soul to Solitude retires,
  Where the WHITE HAND OF MOSES on the Bough
Puts out, and Jesus from the Ground suspires.

V

Eram indeed is gone with all his Rose,
And Jamshid's Sev'n-ring'd Cup where no one knows;
  But still a Ruby kindles in the Vine,
And many a Garden by the Water blows.

VI

And David's lips are lockt; but in divine
High-piping Pahlavi, with 'Wine! Wine! Wine!
  Red Wine!'–the Nightingale cries to the Rose,
That sallow cheek of her's to'incarnadine.

Mas'oud Honarkar, Safavid school, 13.5×22 cm., 2001

Mas'oud Honarkar, Safavid school, 18×11 cm., 1991

VII

Come, fill the Cup, and in the fire of Spring
Your Winter-garment of Repentance fling:
The Bird of Time has but a little way
To flutter –and the Bird is on the Wing.

VIII

Whether at Naishapur or Babylon,
Whether the Cup with sweet or bitter run,
The Wine of Life keeps oozing drop by drop,
The Leaves of Life keep falling one by one.

IX

Each Morn a thousand Roses brings, you say:
Yes, but where leaves the Rose of Yesterday?
And this first Summer month that brings the Rose
Shall take Jamshid and Kaiqobad away.

X

Well, let it take them! What have we to do
With Kaiqobad the Great, or Kaikhosrow?
Let Zal and Rostam bluster as they will,
Or Hatam call to Supper –heed not you.

XI

With me along the strip of Herbage strown
That just divides the desert from the sown,
Where name of Slave and Sultan is forgot–
And Peace to Mahmoud on his golden Throne!

XII

A Book of Verses underneath the Bough,
A Jug of Wine, a Loaf of Bread –and Thou
Beside me singing in the Wilderness–
Oh, Wilderness were Paradise enow!

XIII

Some for the Glories of This World; and some
Sigh for the Prophet's Paradise to come;
   Ah, take the Cash, and let the Credit go,
Nor heed the rumble of a distant Drum!

XIV

Look to the blowing Rose about us —'Lo,
Laughing,' she says, 'into the world I blow,
   At once the silken tassel of my Purse
Tear, and its Treasure on the Garden throw.'

XV

And those who husbanded the Golden grain,
And those who flung it to the winds like Rain,
   Alike to no such aureate Earth are turn'd
As, buried once, Men want dug up again.

XVI

The Worldly Hope men set their Hearts upon
Turns Ashes —or it prospers; and anon,
   Like Snow upon the Desert's dusty Face,
Lighting a little hour or two —was gone.

XVII

Think, in this batter'd Caravanserai
Whose Portals are alternate Night and Day,
   How Sultan after Sultan with his Pomp
Abode his destin'd Hour, and went his way.

XVIII

They say the Lion and the Lizard keep
The Courts where Jamshid gloried and drank deep:
   And Bahram, that great Hunter—the Wild Ass
Stamps o'er his Head, but cannot break his Sleep.

XIX

I sometimes think that never blows so red
The Rose as where some buried Caesar bled;
  That every Hyacinth the Garden wears
Dropt in her Lap from some once lovely Head.

XX

And this reviving Herb whose tender Green
Fledges the River-Lip on which we lean–
  Ah, lean upon it lightly! for who knows
From what once lovely Lip it springs unseen!

XXI

Ah, my Belovéd, fill the Cup that clears
TO-DAY of past Regret and future Fears
  To-morrow!–Why, To-morrow I may be
Myself with Yesterday's Sev'n thousand Years.

XXII

For some we loved, the loveliest and the best
That from his Vintage rolling Time hath prest,
  Have drunk their Cup a Round or two before,
And one by one crept silently to rest.

XXIII

And we, that now make merry in the Room
They left, and Summer dresses in new bloom,
  Ourselves must we beneath the Couch of Earth
Descend –ourselves to make a Couch –for whom?

XXIV

Ah, make the most of what we yet may spend,
Before we too into the Dust descend:
  Dust into Dust, and under Dust, to lie,
Sans Wine, sans Song, sans Singer, and –sans End!

XXV

Alike for those who for TO-DAY prepare,
And those that after some TO-MORROW stare,
A Muezzin from the Tower of Darkness cries:
'Fools! your Reward is neither Here nor There.'

XXVI

Why, all the Saints and Sages who discuss'd
Of the Two Worlds so wisely —they are thrust
Like foolish Prophets forth; their Words to Scorn
Are scatter'd, and their Mouths are stopt with Dust.

XXVII

Myself when young did eagerly frequent
Doctor and Saint, and heard great argument
About it and about: but evermore
Came out by the same door where in I went.

XXVIII

With them the seed of Wisdom did I sow,
And with mine own hand wrought to make it grow;
And this was all the Harvest that I reap'd:
'I came like Water, and like Wind I go.'

XXIX

Into this Universe, and *Why* not knowing
Nor *Whence*, like Water willy-nilly flowing;
And out of it, as Wind along the Waste,
I know not *Whither*, willy-nilly blowing.

XXX

What, without asking, hither hurried *Whence*?
And, without asking, *Whither* hurried hence!
Oh, many a Cup of this forbidden Wine
Must drown the memory of that insolence!

XXXI

Up from Earth's Centre through the Seventh Gate
I rose, and on the Throne of Saturn sate,
   And many a Knot unravel'd by the Road;
But not the Master-knot of Human Fate.

XXXII

There was the Door to which I found no Key;
There was the Veil through which I might not see:
   Some little talk awhile of ME and THEE
There was —and then no more of THEE and ME.

XXXIII

Earth could not answer; nor the Seas that mourn
In flowing Purple, of their Lord forlorn;
   Nor rolling Heaven, with all his Signs reveal'd
And hidden by the sleeve of Night and Morn.

XXXIV

Then of the THEE IN ME who works behind
The Veil, I lifted up my hands to find
   A Lamp amid the Darkness; and I heard,
As from Without: 'THE ME WITHIN THEE BLIND!'

XXXV

Then to the Lip of this poor earthern Urn
I lean'd, the Secret of my Life to learn:
   And Lip to Lip it murmur'd: 'While you live,
Drink! —for, once dead, you never shall return.'

XXXVI

I think the Vessel, that with fugitive
Articulation answer'd, once did live,
   And drink; and Ah! the passive Lip I kiss'd,
How many Kisses might it take —and give!

XXXVII

For I remember stopping by the way
To watch a Potter thumping his wet Clay:
   And with its all-obliterated Tongue
It murmur'd: 'Gently, Brother, gently, pray!'

XXXVIII

And has not such a Story from of Old
Down Man's successive generations roll'd,
   Of such a clod of saturated Earth
Cast by the Maker into Human mould?

XXXIX

And not a drop that from our Cups we throw
For Earth to drink of, but may steal below
   To quench the fire of Anguish in some Eye
There hidden —far beneath, and long ago.

XL

As then the Tulip for her morning sup
Of Heav'nly Vintage from the soil looks up,
   Do you devoutly do the like, till Heav'n
To Earth invert you —like an empty Cup.

XLI

Perplext no more with Human or Divine,
To-morrow's tangle to the winds resign,
   And lose your fingers in the tresses of
The Cypress-slender Minister of Wine.

XLII

And if the Wine you drink, the Lip you press,
End in what All begins and ends in —Yes;
   Think then you are TO-DAY what YESTERDAY
You were —TO-MORROW you shall not be less.

XLIII

So when the Angel of the darker Drink
At last shall find you by the river-brink,
  And, offering his Cup, invite your Soul
Forth to your Lips to quaff—you shall not shrink.

XLIV

Why, if the Soul can fling the Dust aside,
And naked on the Air of Heaven ride,
  Wer't not a Shame—wer't not a Shame for him
In this clay carcase crippled to abide?

XLV

'Tis but a Tent where takes his one day's rest
A Sultan to the realm of Death addrest;
  The Sultan rises, and the dark Ferrash
Strikes, and prepares it for another Guest.

XLVI

And fear not lest Existence closing your
Account, and mine, should know the like no more:
  The Eternal Saki from that Bowl has pour'd
Millions of Bubbles like us, and will pour.

XLVII

When You and I behind the Veil are past,
Oh, but the long, long while the World shall last,
  Which of our Coming and Departure heeds
As the Sea's self should heed a pebble-cast.

XLVIII

A Moment's Halt—a momentary taste
Of BEING from the Well amid the Waste—
  And Lo!—the phantom Caravan has reacht
The NOTHING it set out from—Oh, make haste!

XLIX

Would you that spangle of Existence spend
About THE SECRET--quick about it, Friend!
A Hair perhaps divides the False and True–
And upon what, prithee, does life depend?

L

A Hair perhaps divides the False and True;
Yes; and a single Alif were the clue–
Could you but find it–to the Treasure-house,
And peradventure to THE MASTER too;

LI

Whose secret Presence, through Creation's veins
Running Quicksilver-like eludes your pains;
Taking all shapes from Mah to Mahi; and
They change and perish all–but He remains;

LII

A moment guess'd–then back behind the Fold
Immerst of Darkness round the Drama roll'd
Which, for the Pastime of Eternity,
He doth Himself contrive, enact, behold.

LIII

But if in vain, down on the stubborn floor
Of Earth, and up to Heav'n's unopening Door,
You gaze TO-DAY, while You are You –how then
TO-MORROW, You when shall be You no more?

LIV

Waste not your Hour, nor in the vain pursuit
Of This and That endeavour and dispute;
Better be jocund with the fruitful Grape
Than sadden after none, or bitter, Fruit.

LV

You know, my Friends, with what a brave Carouse
I made a Second Marriage in my house;
Divorced old barren Reason from my Bed,
And took the Daughter of the Vine to Spouse.

LVI

For 'Is' and 'IS-NOT' though with Rule and Line,
And 'UP-AND-DOWN' by Logic I define,
Of all that one should care to fathom I
Was never deep in anything but —Wine.

LVII

Ah, but my Computations, People say,
Reduced the Year to better reckoning? —Nay,
'Twas only striking from the Calendar
Unborn To-morrow, and dead Yesterday.

LVIII

And laterly, by the Tavern Door agape,
Came shining through the Dusk an Angel Shape
Bearing a Vessel on his Shoulder; and
He bid me taste of it; and 'twas —the Grape!

LIX

The Grape that can with Logic absolute
The Two-and-Seventy jarring Sects confute:
The sovereign Alchemist that in a trice
Life's leaden metal into Gold transmute:

LX

The mighty Mahmoud, Allah-breathing Lord,
That all the misbelieving and black Horde
Of Fears and Sorrows that infest the Soul
Scatters before him with his whirlwind Sword.

LXI

Why, be this Juice the growth of God, who dare
Blaspheme the twisted tendril as a Snare?
   A Blessing, we should use it, should we not?
And if a Curse —why, then, Who set it there?

LXII

I must abjure the Balm of Life, I must,
Scared by some After-reckoning ta'en on trust,
   Or lured with Hope of some Diviner Drink
To fill the Cup —when crumbled into Dust!

LXIII

Oh threats of Hell and Hopes of Paradise!
One thing at least is certain—*This* Life flies;
   One thing is certain and the rest is Lies:
The Flower that once has blown for ever dies.

LXIV

Strange, is it not? that of the myriads who
Before us pass'd the door of Darkness through,
   Not one returns to tell us of the Road,
Which to discover we must travel too.

LXV

The Revelations of Devout and Learn'd
Who rose before us, and as Prophets burn'd,
   Are all but Stories, which, awoke from Sleep,
They told their comrades, and to Sleep return'd.

LXVI

I sent my Soul through the Invisible,
Some letter of that After-life to spell:
   And by and by my Soul return'd to me,
And answer'd: 'I Myself am Heav'n and Hell':

LXVII

Heav'n but the Vision of fulfill'd Desire,
And Hell the Shadow from a Soul on fire
  Cast on the Darkness into which Ourselves,
So late emerg'd from, shall so soon expire.

LXVIII

We are no other than a moving row
Of Magic Shadow-shapes that come and go
  Round with the Sun-illumin'd Lantern held
In Midnight by the Master of the Show;

LXIX

But helpless Pieces of the Game He plays
Upon this Chequer-board of Nights and Days;
  Hither and thither moves, and checks, and slays,
And one by one back in the Closet lays.

LXX

The Ball no question makes of Ayes and Noes,
But Here or There as strikes the Player goes:
  And He that toss'd you down into the Field,
He knows about it all —HE knows— HE knows!

LXXI

The Moving Finger writes; and, having writ,
Moves on: nor all your Piety nor Wit
  Shall lure it back to cancel half a Line,
Nor all your Tears wash out a Word of it.

LXXII

And that inverted Bowl they call the Sky,
Whereunder crawling coop'd we live and die,
  Lift not your hands to *It* for help —for It
As impotently moves as you or I.

LXXIII

With Earth's first Clay They did the Last Man knead,
And there of the Last Harvest sow'd the Seed:
And the first Morning of Creation wrote
What the Last Dawn of Reckoning shall read.

LXXIV

YESTERDAY *This* Day's Madness did prepare;
TO-MORROW'S Silence, Triumph, or Despair:
Drink! for you know not whence you came, nor why
Drink! for you know not why you go, nor where.

LXXV

I tell you this —When, started from the Goal,
Over the flaming shoulders of the Foal
Of Heav'n Parwin and Mushtari they flung,
In my predestin'd Plot of Dust and Soul

LXXVI

The Vine had struck a fibre: which about
If clings my Being —let the Dervish flout;
Of my Base metal may be filed a Key,
That shall unlock the Door he howls without.

LXXVII

And this I know: whether the one True Light
Kindle to Love, or Wrath-consume me quite,
One Flash of It within the Tavern caught
Better than in the Temple lost outright.

LXXVIII

What! out of senseless Nothing to provoke
A conscious Something to resent the yoke
Of unpermitted Pleasure, under pain
Of Everlasting Penalties, if broke!

LXXIX

What! from his helpless Creature be repaid
Pure Gold for what he lent him dross-allay'd–
Sue for a Debt we never did contract,
And cannot answer–Oh, the sorry trade!

LXXX

O Thou, who didst with pitfall and with gin
Beset the Road I was to wander in,
Thou wilt not with Predestin'd Evil round
Enmesh, and then impute my Fall to Sin!

LXXXI

O Thou, who Man of baser Earth didst make
And ev'n with Paradise devise the Snake:
For all the Sin wherewith the Face of Man
Is blacken'd–Man's forgiveness give–and take!

.....

LXXXII

As under cover of departing Day
Slunk hunger-stricken Ramazan away,
once more within the Potter's house alone
I stood, surrounded by the Shapes of Clay.

LXXXIII

Shapes of all Sorts and Sizes, great and small,
That stood along the floor and by the wall;
And some loquacious Vessels were; and some
Listen'd perhaps, but never talk'd at all.

LXXXIV

Said one among them: 'Surely not in vain
My substance of the common Earth was ta'en
And to this Figure moulded, to be broke,
Or trampled back to shapeless Earth again.'

LXXXV

Then said a Second: 'Ne'er a peevish Boy
Would break the Bowl from which he drank in joy;
  And He that with his hand the Vessel made
Will surely not in after Wrath destroy.'

LXXXVI

After a momentary silence spake
Some Vessel of a more ungainly Make:
  'They sneer at me for leaning all awry:
What! did the Hand then of the Potter shake?'

LXXXVII

Whereat some one of the loquacious Lot—
I think a Sufi pipkin —waxing hot:
  'All this of Pot and Potter —Tell me, then,
Who is the Potter, pray, and who the Pot?'

LXXXVIII

'Why,' said another, 'Some there are who tell
Of one who threatens he will toss to Hell
  The luckless Pots he marr'd in making —Pish!
He's a Good Fellow, and 'twill all be well.'

LXXXIX

'Well,' murmur'd one, 'Let whoso make or buy,
My Clay with long Oblivion is gone dry:
  But fill me with the old familiar Juice,
Methinks I might recover by and by.'

XC

So while the Vessels one by one were speaking,
The little Moon look'd in that all were seeking:
  And then they jogg'd each other: 'Brother! Brother!
Now for the Porter's shoulder-knot a-creaking!'

......

XCI

Ah, with the Grape my fading Life provide,
And wash the Body whence the Life has died,
And lay me, shrouded in the living Leaf,
By some not unfrequented Garden-side.

XCII

That ev'n my buried Ashes such a snare
Of Vintage shall fling up into the Air,
As not a True believer passing by
But shall be overtaken unaware.

XCIII

Indeed the Idols I have loved so long
Have done my credit in this World much wrong:
Have drown'd my Glory in a shallow Cup,
And sold my Reputation for a Song.

XCIV

Indeed, indeed, Repentance oft before
I swore —but was I sober when I swore?
And then and then came Spring, and Rose-in-hand
My threadbare Penitence apieces tore.

XCV

And much as Wine has play'd the Infidel,
And robb'd me of my Robe of Honour —Well,
I wonder often what the Vintners buy
One half so precious as the stuff they sell.

XCVI

Yet Ah, that Spring should vanish with the Rose!
That Youth's sweet-scented manuscript should close!
The Nightingale that in the branches sang,
Ah whence, and whither flown again, who knows!

XCVII

Would but the Desert of the Fountain yield
One glimpse —if dimly, yet indeed reveal'd,
   To which the fainting Traveller might spring,
As springs the trampled herbage of the field!

XCVIII

Would but some winged Angel ere too late
Arrest the yet unfolded Roll of Fate,
   And make the stern Recorder otherwise
Enregister, or quite obliterate!

XCIX

Ah Love! could you and I with Him conspire
To grasp this sorry Scheme of Things entire,
   Would not we shatter it to bits—and then
Remould it nearer to the Heart's Desire!

C

Yon rising Moon that looks for us again—
How oft hereafter will she wax and wane;
   How oft hereafter rising look for us
Through this same Garden—and for *one* in vain!

CI

And when like her, O Saki, you shall pass
Among the Guests Star-scatter'd on the Grass,
   And in your joyous errand reach the spot
Where I made One —turn down an empty Glass!

Mas'oud Honarkar, Safavid school, 20×70 cm., 2001

Mas'oud Honarkar, Safavid school, 15×22 cm., 2002

RUMI

1

Time bringeth swift to end
The rout men keep;
Death's wolf is nigh to rend
These silly sheep.

See, how in pride they go
With lifted head,
Till Fate with a sudden blow
Smiteth them dead.

2

Thou who lovest, like a crow,
Winter's chill and winter's snow,
Ever exiled from the vale's
Roses red, and nightingales:

Take this moment to thy heart!
When the moment shall depart,
Long thou 'lt seek it as it flies
With a hundred lamps and eyes.

3

The heavenly rider passed;
The dust rose in the air;
He sped; but the dust he cast
Yet hangeth there.

Straight forward thy vision be,
And gaze not left or right;
His dust is here, and he
In the Infinite.

4

Who was he that said
The immortal spirit is dead,
Or how dared he say
Hope's sun hath passed away?

An enemy of the sun,
Standing his roof upon,
Bound up both his eyes
And cried: 'Lo, the sun dies!'

5

'Who lifteth up the spirit,
Say, who is he?'
'Who gave in the beginning
This life to me.

Who hoodeth, like a falcon's,
Awhile mine eyes,
But presently shall loose me
To hunt my prize.'

6

As salt resolved in the ocean
I was swallowed in God's sea,
Past faith, past unbelieving,
Past doubt, past certainty.

Suddenly in my bosom
A star shone clear and bright;
All the suns of heaven
Vanished in that star's light.

7

Flowers every night
Blossom in the sky;
Peace in the Infinite;
At peace am I.

Sighs a hundredfold
From my heart arise;
My heart, dark and cold,
Flames with my sighs.

8

He that is my soul's repose
Round my heart encircling goes,
Round my heart and soul of bliss
He encircling is.

Laughing, from my earthy bed
Like a tree I lift my head,
For the Fount of living mirth
Washes round my earth.

9

The breeze of the morn
Scatters musk in its train,
Fragrance borne
From my fair love's lane.

Ere the world wastes,
Sleep no more: arise!
The caravan hastes,
The sweet scent dies.

10

If life be gone, fresh life to you
God offereth,
A life eternal, to renew
This life of death.

The Fount of Immortality
In Love is found;
Then come, and in this boundless sea
Of Love be drowned.

11

Happy was I
In the pearl's heart to lie;
Till, lashed by life's hurricane,
Like a tossed wave I ran.

The secret of the sea
I uttered thunderously;
Like a spent cloud on the shore
I slept, and stirred no more.

12

He set the world aflame,
And laid me on the same;
A hundred tongues of fire
Lapped round my pyre.

And when the blazing tide
Engulfed me, and I sighed,
Upon my mouth in haste
His hand He placed.

13

Though every way I try
His whim to satisfy,
His every answering word
Is a pointed sword.

See how the blood drips
From His finger-tips;
Why does He find it good
To wash in my blood?

14

Remembering Thy lip,
The ruby red I kiss;
Having not that to sip,
My lips press this.

Not to Thy far sky
Reaches my stretched hand,
Wherefore, kneeling, I
Embrace the land.

15

I sought a soul in the sea
And found a coral there;
Beneath the foam for me
An ocean was all laid bare.

Into my heart's night
Along a narrow way
I groped; and lo! the light,
An infinite land of day.

A. J. Arberry.

LYRIC

SANA'I

GOOD NIGHT

Darling, my heart I gave to thee–
    Good night!   I go.
Thou know'st my heartfelt sympathy–
    Good night!   I go.
Should I behold thee ne'er again
    'Tis right, 'tis right;
I clasp this Hour of Parting tight–
    Good night!   I go.
With raven tress and visage clear,
    Enchantress dear,
Hast made my daylight dark and drear:
    Good night!   I go.
Oh Light of Faith thy Face, thy hair
    Like Doubt's Despair:
Both this and that yield torment rare–
    Good night!   I go.
Therefore 'twixt Fire and Water me
    Thou thus dost see,
Lips parched and dry, tear-raining eye:
    Good night!   I go.

E. G. Browne.

THY LOVE

That heart which stands aloof from pain and woe
No seal or signature of Love can show:
Thy Love, thy Love I chose, and as for wealth,
If wealth be not my portion, be it so!
For wealth, I ween, pertaineth to the World;
Ne'er can the World and Love together go!
So long as Thou dost dwell within my heart
Ne'er can my heart become the thrall of Woe.

E. G. Browne.

THE DEVIL'S COMPLAINT

He was my only passion,
 All other loves apart;
The phoenix of devotion
 Nested within my heart.

About my court battalions
 Of angels gathered nigh,
My threshold was exalted
 Beyond the heavens high.

Upon my way (Oh cunning)
 A hidden snare He set,
And there within its circle
 Laid Adam for a bait.

To brand me as accursed—
 This was His secret aim,
And Adam was the pretext;
 And He achieved the same.

A heavenly preceptor
 Above the clouds was I;
In Paradise my hope was
 To dwell eternally.

I paid Him loyal service
 For many a thousand year,
And laid up countless treasure
 Of piety sincere.

I read upon the Tablet
 The curse should fall on one;
Of all I had suspicion:
 It was for me alone.

Of Earth was Adam's substance,
And mine of Light refined;
'I am the One,' I reasoned;
But he was the designed.

'Thou didst not make obeisance':
So all the angels said;
But with this thing between us
How could I bow my head?

A. J. Arberry.

PERFECT LOVE

Who would be loved, let him possess
A true beloved like mine,
And share in secret blessedness
Love's mystery divine:
Lovers like us none else, I guess,
Are found in earth's confine.

'Soul of the world' —such was the name
My idol gave to me;
While I do live, her I proclaim
Soul of my world to be,
And none I know doth own the same
Dear loyalty as she.

Behold me now —take not as heard,
But ask, and all will say
That this is sooth: this was her word:
'I shall be thine for aye.'
Truly she is, as she averred,
And I am hers alway.

A. J. Arberry.

ATTAR

THE VEIL

We are the Magians of old,
Islam is not the faith we hold;
In irreligion is our fame,
And we have made our creed a shame.

Now to the tavern we repair
To gamble all our substance there,
Now in the monastery cell
We worship with the infidel.

When Satan chances us to see
He doffs his cap respectfully,
For we have lessons to impart
To Satan in the tempter's art.

We were not in such nature made
Of any man to be afraid;
Head and foot in naked pride
Like sultans o'er the earth we ride.

But we, alas, aweary are
And the road is very far;
We know not by what way to come
Unto the place that is our home.

And therefore we are in despair
How to order our affair
Because, wherever we have sought,
Our minds were utterly distraught.

When shall it come to pass, ah when,
That suddenly, beyond our ken,
We shall succeed to rend this veil
That doth our whole affair conceal?

What veil soever after this
Apparent to our vision is,
With the flame of knowledge true
We shall consume it through and through.

Where at the first in that far place
We came into the world of space,
Our soul by travail in the end
To that perfection shall ascend.

And so shall Attar shattered be
And, rapt in sudden ecstasy,
Soar to godly vision, even
Beyond the veils of earth and heaven.

A. J. Arberry.

CHRISTIAN CHILD

A Christian child of grace divine,
And in his hand the purple wine—
So fair a sight, in very truth,
As love is in the time of youth,
Eager as fire, and all agleam,
Fresh as that everlasting stream
Last night he came, and sat him down.
A girdle circleted his gown;
His lips were parted in a smile
Glittering sweet; yet all the while
A hundred worlds of faithlessness
Hung hidden in each fatal tress.
He came within, and sat at rest,
And put our elder to the test;
Who took a glass, and liked it well,
And bade his faith a long farewell.
Dear God, how swift and suddenly
Fate strikes! A man so wise as he—
Alas, that he should yield the day
To one so foolish and so gay!

For when our elder viewed his face,
Helplessly rooted to the place
He called the Christian child, and said:
'Come, tell me what is in thy head.'
'The sign of love,' said he, 'is this:
That thou can neither be, nor is.'
Hearing, the sage his life did give:
Attar, tell thou, for thou dost live!

A. J. Arberry.

RUMI

POOR COPIES

Poor copies out of heaven's original,
Pale earthly pictures mouldering to decay,
What care although your beauties break and fall,
When that which gave them life endures for aye?

Oh, never vex thine heart with idle woes:
All high discourse enchanting the rapt ear,
All gilded landscapes and brave glistering shows
Fade —perish, but it is not as we fear.

Whilst far away the living fountains ply,
Each petty brook goes brimful to the main
Since brook nor fountain can for ever die,
Thy fears how foolish, thy lament how vain!

What is this fountain, wouldst thou rightly know?
The Soul whence issue all created things.
Doubtless the rivers shall not cease to flow,
Till silenced are the everlasting springs.

Farewell to sorrow, and with quiet mind
Drink long and deep: let others fondly deem
The channel empty they perchance may find,
Or fathom that unfathomable stream.

The moment thou to this low world wast given,
A ladder stood whereby thou might'st aspire;
And first thy steps, which upward still have striven,
From mineral mounted to the plant; then higher

To animal existence; next, the Man,
With knowledge, reason, faith. Oh wondrous goal!
This body, which a crumb of dust began—
How fairly fashioned the consummate whole!

Yet stay not here thy journey: thou shalt grow
An angel bright and home far off in heaven.
Plod on, plunge last in the great Sea, that so
Thy little drop make oceans seven times seven.

'The Son of God!' Nay, leave that word unsaid,
Say: 'God is One, the pure, the single Truth.'
What though thy frame be withered, old, and dead,
If the soul keep her fresh immortal youth?

R. A. Nicholson.

DEPARTURE

Up, O ye lovers, and away! 'Tis time to leave the world for aye.
Hark, loud and clear from heaven the drum of parting calls – let none delay!
The cameleer hath risen amain, made ready all the camel-train,
And quittance now desires to gain: why sleep ye, travellers, I pray?
Behind us and before there swells the din of parting and of bells;
To shoreless space each moment sails a disembodied spirit away.
From yonder starry lights, and through those curtain-awnings darkly blue,

Mysterious figures float in view, all strange and secret things display.
From this orb, wheeling round its pole, a wondrous slumber o'er thee stole:
O weary life that weighest naught, O sleep that on my soul dost weigh!
O heart, toward thy heart's love wend, and O friend, fly toward the Friend,
Be wakeful, watchman, to the end: drowse seemingly no watch man may.

R. A. *Nicholson.*

HE COMES

He comes, a moon whose like the sky ne'er saw, awake or dreaming,
Crowned with eternal flame no flood can lay.
Lo, from the flagon of thy love, O Lord, my soul is swimming,
And ruined all my body's house of clay!

When first the Giver of the grape my lonely heart befriended,
Wine fired my bosom and my veins filled up;
But when his image all mine eye possessed, a voice descended:
'Well done, O sovereign Wine and peerless Cup!'

Love's mighty arm from roof to base each dark abode is hewing,
Where chinks reluctant catch a golden ray.
My heart, when Love's sea of a sudden burst into its viewing,
Leaped headlong in, with 'Find me now who may!'

As, the sun moving, clouds behind him run,
All hearts attend thee, O Tabriz's Sun!

R. A. *Nicholson.*

Mas'oud Honarkar, Safavid school, 22×32 cm., 2002

Mas'oud Honarkar, Safavid school, 20×14 cm., 2003

DESCENT

I made a far journey
Earth's fair cities to view,
But like to love's city
City none I knew.

At the first I knew not
That city's worth,
And turned in my folly
A wanderer on earth.

From so sweet a country
I must needs pass,
And like to cattle
Grazed on every grass.

As Moses' people
I would liefer eat
Garlic, than manna
And celestial meat.

What voice in this world
To my ear has come
Save the voice of love
Was a tapped drum.

Yet for that drum-tap
From the world of All
Into this perishing
Land I did fall.

That world a lone spirit
Inhabiting,
Like a snake I crept
Without foot or wing.

The wine that was laughter
And grace to sip
Like a rose I tasted
Without throat or lip.

‘Spirit, go a journey,’
Love’s voice said:
’Lo, a home of travail
I have made.’

Much, much I cried:
‘I will not go’;
Yea, and rent my raiment
And made great woe.

Even as now I shrink
To be gone from here,
Even so thence
To part I did fear.

‘Spirit, go thy way,’
Love called again,
‘And I shall be ever nigh thee
As thy neck’s vein.’

Much did love enchant me
And made much guile;
Love’s guile and enchantment
Captured me the while.

In ignorance and folly
When my wings I spread,
From palace unto prison
I was swiftly sped.

Now I would tell
How thither thou mayst come;
But ah, my pen is broken
And I am dumb.

A. J. Arberry.

SA'DI

SHIRAZ

Oh Fortune suffers me not to clasp my sweetheart to my breast,
Nor lets me forget my exile long in a kiss on her sweet lip pressed.
The noose wherewith she is wont to snare her victims far and wide
I will steal away, that so one day I may lure her to my side.
Yet I shall not dare caress her hair with a hand that is overbold,
For snared therein, like birds in a gin, are the hearts of lovers untold.
A slave am I to that gracious form, which, as I picture it,
Is clothed in grace with a measuring-rod, as tailors a garment fit.
Oh cypress-tree, with silver limbs, this colour and scent of thine
Have shamed the scent of the myrtle-plant and the bloom of the eglantine.
Judge with thine eyes, and set thy foot in the garden fair and free,
And tread the jasmine under thy foot, and the flowers of the Judas-tree.
Oh joyous and gay is the New Year's Day, and in Shiraz most of all;
Even the stranger forgets his home, and becomes its willing thrall.
O'er the garden's Egypt, Joseph-like, the fair red rose is King,
And the Zephyr, e'en to the heart of the town, doth the scent of his raiment bring.
Oh wonder not if in time of Spring thou dost rouse such jealousy,
That the cloud doth weep while the flowrets smile, and all on account of thee!
If o'er the dead thy feet should tread, those feet so fair and fleet,
No wonder it were if thou should'st hear a voice from his winding-sheet.
Distraction is banned from this our land in the time of our lord the King,
Save that I am distracted with love of thee, and men with the songs I sing.

E. G. Browne.

WANTONING

The heart that loves with patience —a stone 'tis, not a heart;
Nay, love and patience dwell of old a thousand leagues apart.
O brethren of the mystic path, leave blame and me alone!
Repentance in the way of Love is glass against a stone.
No more in secret need I drink, in secret dance and sing:
For us that love religiously, good name's a shameful thing.
What right and justice should I see or what instruction hear?
Mine eye is to the Saki turned, and to the lute mine ear.
I caught the zephyr's fluttering skirt for sweet remembrance' sake:
Alas, I have ta'en but empty wind where scent I hoped to take.
Who'll bring a message to my Dear that off in anger went?
Go, tell him I have dropped the shield, if he on war is bent;
And let him kill as he knows how! for if no vision there be
Of him, the wide world seems a cramped uneasy place to me.

R. A. *Nicholson.*

DANCE

Lovers' souls 'gin dance with glee
When the zephyr fans thy roses.
Ne'er melts thy stony heart for me,
Mine as a sunk stone heavily
In thy dimple's well reposes.

Life were an offering too small,
Else 'tis easy to surrender
Unto thee, who need'st not call
Painter's art to deck thy wall:
Thou alone dost give it splendour.

Better sicken, better die
At thy feet than live to lose thee.
Pilgrim to Love's sanctuary,
What car'st thou, 'neath desert sky,
How the thorns of Absence bruise thee?

R. A. *Nicholson.*

LOVE THE FOE

When the enemy doth throw
    His lasso,
As his whim determines, so
    We must do.

None has earned, till he has loved,
    Manly fame,
E'en as silver pure is proved
    By the flame.

Never did reformer take
    Passion's way,
But that both worlds he must stake
    In the play.

To his memory I am so
    Wholly turned,
That with self my mind is no
    More concerned.

Thanks to love sincere and whole
    I confess;
Love, that burned my heart, my soul
    Doth caress.

Sa'di! poet sweeter page
    Never writ
For a present to an age
    Great with wit.

May thy sugar tongue remain
    Ever blest,
That hath taught the world such pain
    And unrest.

A. J. Arberry.

JOY AND SORROW

Roses are blossoming
And joyous birds do sing
In such a season gay,
A desert-faring day.

Autumn the scatterer
Setteth the leaves astir;
The painter morning air
Decketh the garden fair.

Yet no desire have I
In grassy meads to lie:
Where'er thou art in sight,
There dwelleth true delight.

Beauty to view, they said,
Is joy prohibited:
Nay, but our view of bliss
Lawful and holy is.

Lo, in thy face I see
Creation's mystery,
As water doth appear
Within a crystal clear.

Whatever man thy love
Seals not his heart above,
No heart is his to own
But flint, and granite stone.

These flames (one of these days)
That neath the cauldron blaze
Will burn me utterly
And make an end of me.

Sa'di's distressful dole
And tears uncountable
(They say) are contrary
To all propriety.

They say; but little those
Who on the shore repose
Know of the woe that we
Bear on the stormy sea.

A. J. Arberry.

HELD FAST

Soul of mine, may my soul
Thy ransom be,
Thou who hast not a friend
In memory!

Thou art gone, and to none
Payest thou heed;
Never fir moved so freely
In the mead.

Grace of God rest on him
Whose loving care
Nurtured thee, and on her
Who did thee bear.

May good chance all thy fondest
Hopes fulfil,
And protect thee from malice
And ill will.

What did He, who thy face
So sweetly drew,
That a world into tumult
Wild He threw?

Once shall I seize my monarch's
 Rein, and say:
'From the fair cruel charmers
 Justice, pray!'

With those eyes slumbrous dark,
 That lily brow,
Nevermore my lost heart
 Returnest thou.

Intellect doth with love
 But ill agree,
Where the slave slays the lord
 Implacably.

He, that had on love's threshold
 Never yet
Laid his foot, there at last
 His brow has set.

Face to dust went; and now
 Not strange it were
If the head, blown by passion,
 Goes to air.

The wild fowl, that did burst
 And break his chain,
In the trap, though so crafty,
 Falls again.

Others weep, whom an alien
 Hand assails;
For the hand of his own love
 Sa'di wails.

'Now,' I said, 'through the world
 I'll wander free,
Break my slave's chains, and go
 In liberty.

'Are there not out of Fars
Homes to be had?
Not in Rum, Sham, or Basra,
Or Bagdad?'

Yet these still hold my garment
By the hem—
Earth of Shiraz, and Rukna's
Silver stream.

A. J. Arberry.

IRAQI

MYSTIC CUPS

Cups are those a-flashing with wine,
or suns through the clouds a-gleaming?
So clear is the wine and the glass so fine
That the two are one in seeming.
The glass is all and the wine is naught,
Or the glass is naught and the wine is all:
Since the air the rays of the sun hath caught
The light combines with night's dark pall,
For the night hath made a truce with the day,
And thereby is ordered the world's array.
If thou know'st not which is day, which night,
Or which is goblet and which is wine,
By wine and cup divine aright
The Water of Life and its secret sign:
Like night and day thou may'st e'en assume
Certain knowledge and doubt's dark gloom.
If these comparisons clear not up
All these problems low and high,
Seek for the world-reflecting cup,
That thou may'st see with reason's eye
That all that is, is He indeed,
Soul and loved one and heart and creed.

E. G. Browne.

I CANNOT SEE

Save love of thee a soul in me I cannot see, I cannot see;
An object for my love save thee I cannot see, I cannot see.
Repose or patience in my mind I cannot find, I cannot find,
While gracious glance or friendship free I cannot see, I cannot see.
Show in thy face some sign of grace, since for the pain wherewith I'm slain
Except thy face a remedy I cannot see, I cannot see.
If thou would'st see me, speed thy feet, for parted from thy presence sweet,
Continued life on earth for me I cannot see, I cannot see.
O friend, stretch out a hand to save, for I am fallen in a wave
Of which the crest, if crest there be, I cannot see, I cannot see.
With gracious care and kindly air come hither and my state repair;
A better state, apart from thee, I cannot see, I cannot see.
Some pathway to Iraqi teach whereby thy gateway he may reach,
For vagrant so bemused as he I cannot see, I cannot see.

Sir Denison Ross.

GAMBLE

When at thy love a lamp we light
Our barn of being is ablaze,
And of that inward glow so bright
A wisp of smoke to heaven we raise.

Turn thou on us thy beauty's sun:
Our day is dark without thy face,
But we are blind to everyone
When we have seen thy matchless grace.

Lo, we have cast, and made our stake;
Our life and heart hang on a spin;
What better throw could gambler make
If, giving all, thy love he win?

Like children, in thy school of love
The alphabet of love we learn;
Along thy path to death I move,
And I am glad; I will not turn.

A. J. Arberry.

AMIR KHOSROW

GODDESS

O Thou whose face,
With envied grace,
The magi's Gods inflames!
Howe'er my verse
Thy praise rehearse,
Still more thy beauty claims.

Sprightly and gay
As fabled fay,
Soft as the roseate leaf!
Say what I will—
Superior still!
Wondrous! beyond belief!

My vagrant eye
Did ne'er descry
A fairer form than thine:
Is it of earth?
Or heavenly birth?
Or Fairy's, half divine?

The world I rov'd,
And frequent lov'd
Those charms which all adore:
Maids who excell'd
I oft beheld—
But thou art something more.

Each soul thy prey,
Each heart thy sway
Avows with mad'ning pain;
Thy magic eyes
Of Nergiss dyes
Idolatry maintain.

Khosrow, fair maid,
Intreats thine aid,
A stranger at thy door;
Oh, in God's name,
Regard the claim
Of strangers who implore.

J. H. Hindley.

HAFEZ

A PERSIAN SONG

Sweet maid, if thou would'st charm my sight,
And bid these arms thy neck infold;
That rosy cheek, that lily hand,
Would give thy poet more delight
Than all Bokhara's vaunted gold,
Than all the gems of Samarqand.

Boy, let yon liquid ruby flow,
And bid thy pensive heart be glad,
Whate'er the frowning zealots say:
Tell them, their Eden cannot show
A stream so clear as Roknabad,
A bower so sweet as Mosalla.

Oh! when these fair perfidious maids,
Whose eyes our secret haunts infest,
Their dear destructive charms display;

Each glance my tender breast invades,
And robs my wounded soul of rest,
As Tartars seize their destin'd prey.

In vain with love our bosoms glow:
Can all our tears, can all our sighs,
New lustre to those charms impart?
Can cheeks, where living roses blow,
Where nature spreads her richest dyes,
Require the borrow'd gloss of art?

Speak not of fate: ah! change the theme,
And talk of odours, talk of wine,
Talk of the flowers that round us bloom:
'Tis all a cloud, 'tis all a dream;
To love and joy thy thoughts confine,
Nor hope to pierce the sacred gloom.

Beauty has such resistless power,
That even the chaste Egyptian dame
Sigh'd for the blooming Hebrew boy:
For her how fatal was the hour
When to the banks of Nilus came
A youth so lovely and so coy!

But ah! sweet maid, my counsel hear
(Youth should attend when those advise
Whom long experience renders sage):
While musick charms the ravish'd ear;
While sparkling cups delight our eyes,
Be gay; and scorn the frowns of age.

What cruel answer have I heard!
And yet, by heaven, I love thee still:
Can aught be cruel from thy lip?
Yet say, how fell that bitter word
From lips which streams of sweetness fill,
Which naught but drops of honey sip?

Go boldly forth, my simple lay,
Whose accents flow with artless ease,
Like orient pearls at random strung:
Thy notes are sweet, the damsels say;
But Oh! far sweeter, if they please
The nymph for whom these notes are sung.

Sir William Jones.

LOVE AND WINE

Fill, fill the cup with sparkling wine,
Deep let me drink the juice divine,
    To soothe my tortur'd heart;
For Love, who seem'd at first so mild,
So gently look'd, so gaily smil'd,
    Here deep has plung'd his dart.

When, sweeter than the damask rose,
From Leila's locks the Zephyr blows,
    How glows my keen desire!
I chide the wanton gale's delay,
I'm jealous of his am'rous play,
    And all my soul's on fire.

To Love the flowing goblet drain,
With wine the sacred carpet stain,
    If your gay host invites;
For he who treads the mazy round
Of mighty Love's enchanted ground,
    Knows all his laws and rites.

But longer, midst the young and fair,
With happy mind and easy air,
    Can I delighted roam?
When, hark; the heart-alarming bell
Proclaims aloud, with dismal knell,
    Depart, thy hour is come!

The night now darkens all around,
Now howl the winds, the waves resound;
    We part to meet no more:
Our dreadful fate how can they know,
Whose tranquil hours unruffl'd flow
    Secure upon the shore?

How many tales does slander frame,
And rumour whisper 'gainst my fame;
    With malice both combine:
Because I wish to pass my days
Despising what each snarler says,
    With friendship, love, and wine.

But, Hafez, if thou would'st enjoy
Ecstatic rapture, soul-felt joy,
    Blest as the powers above,
Snatch to thine arms the blooming maid,
Then, on her charming bosom laid,
    Abandon all for Love.

J. Richardson.

MY BOSOM GRAC'D

My bosom grac'd with each gay flow'r,
    I grasp the bowl, my nymph in glee;
The monarch of the world this hour
    Is but a slave compar'd to me.

Intrude not with the taper's light,
    My social friends, with beaming eyes;
Trundle around a starry night,
    And lo! my nymph the moon supplies.

Away, thy sprinkling odours spare,
    Be not officiously thus kind;
The waving ringlets of my Fair
    Shed perfume to the fainting wind.

My ears th' enlivening notes inspire,
As lute or harp alternate sound;
My eyes those ruby lips admire,
Or catch the glasses sparkling round.

Then let no moments steal away,
Without thy mistress and thy wine;
The spring flowers blossom to decay,
And youth but glows to own decline.

T. Law.

FRIENDLY ZEPHYR

Go, friendly Zephyr! whisp'ring greet
Yon gentle fawn with slender feet;
Say that in quest of her I rove
The dangerous steeps, the wilds of love.

Thou merchant who dost sweetness vend
(Long may kind heav'n thy life defend!),
Ah, why unfriendly thus forget
Thy am'rous sweet-billed parroquet?

Is it, O rose! thy beauty's pride
That casts affection far aside,
Forbidding thee to court the tale
Of thy fond mate, the nightingale?

I know not why 'tis rare to see
The colour of sincerity
In nymphs who boast majestic grace,
Dark eyes, and silver-beaming face.

What tho' that face be angel fair,
One fault does all its beauty mar;
Nor faith, nor constancy adorn
Thy charms, which else might shame the morn.

A lady standing, probably Mirza Nourollah, 19×28 cm., about 1935

A man with a bird in hand, unsigned, 13×18 cm., about 1925, watercolor and gilding on leather

By gentle manners we control
The wise, the sense-illumin'd soul:
No idle lure, no glitt'ring bait
Th' experienc'd bird will captivate.

What wonder, Hafez, that thy strain,
Whose sounds inchant th' ethereal plain,
Should tempt each graver star to move
In dances with the star of love?

J. Nott.

SLAVE

Zephyr, should'st thou chance to rove
By the mansion of my love,
From her locks ambrosial bring
Choicest odours on thy wing.

Could'st thou waft me from her breast
Tender sighs to say I'm blest,
As she lives! my soul would be
Sprinkl'd o'er with ecstasy.

But if Heav'n the boon deny,
Round her stately footsteps fly,
With the dust that thence may rise,
Stop the tears which bathe these eyes.

Lost, poor mendicant! I roam
Begging, craving she would come:
Where shall I thy phantom see,
Where, dear nymph, a glimpse of thee?

Like the wind-tost reed my breast
Fann'd with hope is ne'er at rest,
Throbbing, longing to excess
Her fair figure to caress.

Yes, my charmer, tho' I see
Thy heart courts no love with me,
Not for worlds, could they be mine,
Would I give a hair of thine.

Why, O care! shall I in vain
Strive to shun thy galling chain,
When these strains still fail to save,
And make Hafez more a slave.

J. H. Hindley.

THE LESSON OF THE FLOWERS

'Twas morning, and the Lord of day
    Had shed his light o'er Shiraz' towers,
Where bulbuls trill their love-lorn lay
    To serenade the maiden flowers.

Like them, oppressed by love's sweet pain
    I wander in a garden fair;
And there, to cool my throbbing brain,
    I woo the perfumed morning air.

The damask rose with beauty gleams,
    Its face all bathed in ruddy light,
And shines like some bright star that beams
    From out the sombre veil of night.

The very bulbul, as the glow
    Of pride and passion warms its breast,
Forgets awhile its former woe
    In pride that conquers love's unrest.

The sweet narcissus opes its eye,
    A tear-drop glistening on the lash,
As though 'twere gazing piteously
    Upon the tulip's bleeding gash.

The lily seemed to menace me,
   And showed its curved and quivering blade,
While every frail anemone
   A gossip's open mouth displayed.

And here and there a graceful group
   Of flowers, like men who worship wine,
Each raising up his little stoup
   To catch the dew-drop's draught divine.

And others yet like Hebes stand,
   Their dripping vases downward turned,
As if dispensing to the band
   The wine for which their hearts had burned.

This moral it is mine to sing:
   Go learn a lesson of the flowers;
Joy's season is in life's young spring,
   Then seize, like them, the fleeting hours.

E. H. Palmer.

ROSE BLOOM

The rose has flushed red, the bud has burst,
And drunk with joy is the nightingale–
Hail, Sufis! lovers of wine, all hail!
For wine is proclaimed to a world athirst.
Like a rock your repentance seemed to you;
Behold the marvel! of what avail
Was your rock, for a goblet has cleft it in two!

Bring wine for the king and the slave at the gate!
Alike for all is the banquet spread,
And drunk and sober are warmed and fed.
When the feast is done and the night grows late,
And the second door of the tavern gapes wide,
The low and the mighty must bow the head
'Neath the archway of Life, to meet what ... outside?

Except thy road through affliction pass,
None may reach the halting-station of mirth;
God's treaty: Am I not Lord of the earth?
Man sealed with a sigh: Ah yes, alas!
Nor with Is nor Is Not let thy mind contend;
Rest assured all perfection of mortal birth
In the great Is Not at the last shall end.

For Assaf's pomp, and the steeds of the wind,
And the speech of birds, down the wind have fled,
And he that was lord of them all is dead;
Of his mastery nothing remains behind.
Shoot not thy feathered arrow astray!
A bowshot's length through the air it has sped,
And then ... dropped down in the dusty way.

But to thee, O Hafez, to thee, O Tongue
That speaks through the mouth of the slender reed,
What thanks to thee when thy verses speed
From lip to lip, and the song thou hast sung?

Gertrude Bell.

COMFORT

The secret draught of wine and love repressed
Are joys foundationless–then come whate'er
May come, slave to the grape I stand confessed!
Unloose, O friend, the knot of thy heart's care,
Despite the warning that the Heavens reveal!
For all his thought, never astronomer
That loosed the knot of Fate those Heavens conceal!

Not all the changes that thy days unfold
Shall rouse thy wonder; Time's revolving sphere
Over a thousand lives like thine has rolled.
That cup within thy fingers, dost not hear
The voices of dead kings speak through the clay?
Qobad, Bahman, Jamshid, their dust is here.
'Gently upon me set thy lips!' they say.

What man can tell where Kavous and Kai have gone?
Who knows where even now the restless wind
Scatters the dust of Jam's imperial throne?
And where the tulip, following close behind
The feet of Spring, her scarlet chalice rears,
There Farhad for the love of Shirin pined,
Dyeing the desert red with his heart's tears.

Bring, bring the cup! drink we while yet we may
To our soul's ruin the forbidden draught;
Perhaps a treasure-trove is hid away
Among those ruins where the wine has laughed!—
Perhaps the tulip knows the fickleness
Of Fortune's smile, for on her stalk's green shaft
She bears a wine-cup through the wilderness.

The murmuring stream of Roknabad, the breeze
That blows from out Mosalla's fair pleasaunce,
Summon me back when I would seek heart's ease,
Travelling afar; what though Love's countenance
Be turned full harsh and sorrowful on me,
I care not so that Time's unfriendly glance
Still from my Lady's beauty turnéd be.

Like Hafez, drain the goblet cheerfully
While minstrels touch the lute and sweetly sing,
For all that makes thy heart rejoice in thee
Hangs of Life's single, slender, silken string.

Gertrude Bell.

DESIRE

I cease not from desire till my desire
Is satisfied; or let my mouth attain
My love's red mouth, or let my soul expire,
Sighed from those lips that sought her lips in vain.
Others may find another love as fair;
Upon her threshold I have laid my head:
The dust shall cover me, still lying there,
When from my body life and love have fled.

My soul is on my lips ready to fly,
But grief beats in my heart and will not cease,
Because not once, not once before I die,
Will her sweet lips give all my longing peace.
My breath is narrowed down to one long sigh
For a red mouth that burns my thoughts like fire;
When will that mouth draw near and make reply
To one whose life is straitened with desire?

When I am dead, open my grave and see
The cloud of smoke that rises round thy feet:
In my dead heart the fire still burns for thee;
Yea, the smoke rises from my winding-sheet!
Ah come, Beloved! for the meadows wait
Thy coming, and the thorn bears flowers instead
Of thorns, the cypress fruit, and desolate
Bare winter from before thy steps has fled.

Hoping within some garden ground to find
A red rose soft and sweet as thy soft cheek
Through every meadow blows the western wind,
Through every garden he is fain to seek.
Reveal thy face! that the whole world may be
Bewildered by thy radiant loveliness;
The cry of man and woman comes to thee,
Open thy lips and comfort their distress!

Each curling lock of thy luxuriant hair
Breaks into barbéd hooks to catch my heart,
My broken heart is wounded everywhere
With countless wounds from which the red drops
start.
Yet when sad lovers meet and tell their sighs,
Not without praise shall Hafez' name be said,
Not without tears, in those pale companies
Where joy has been forgot and hope has fled.

Gertrude Bell.

TIDINGS OF UNION

Where are the tidings of union? that I may arise—
Forth from the dust I will rise up to welcome thee!
My soul, like a homing bird, yearning for Paradise,
Shall arise and soar, from the snares of the world set free.
When the voice of thy love shall call me to be thy slave,
I shall rise to a greater far than the mastery
Of life and the living, time and the mortal span:
Pour down, O Lord! from the clouds of thy guiding grace
The rain of a mercy that quickeneth on my grave,
Before, like dust that the wind bears from place to place,
I arise and flee beyond the knowledge of man.
When to my grave thou turnest thy blessed feet,
Wine and the lute thou shalt bring in thine hand to me,
Thy voice shall ring through the folds of my winding-sheet,
And I will arise and dance to thy minstrelsy.
Though I be old, clasp me one night to thy breast,
And I, when the dawn shall come to awaken me,
With the flush of youth on my cheek from thy bosom will rise.
Rise up! let mine eyes delight in thy stately grace!
Thou art the goal to which all men's endeavour has pressed,
And thou the idol of Hafez' worship; thy face
From the world and life shall bid him come forth and arise!

Gertrude Bell.

LAWFUL WINE

Rang through the dim tavern a voice yesterday:
'Pardon for sins! Drinkers of wine, drink! Ye may!'

Such was the word; hear the good news, Angel-borne;
Mercy divine still to the end holds its way.

Great are our sins; greater is God's grace than all;
Deep are his hid counsels, and who says them nay?

Bear her away, Reason the Dull, tavernwards,
There shall the red wine set her pale veins a-play.

Union with Him strife or essay forceth not;
Yet, O my heart, e'en to the full, strive, essay.

Still is my ear ringed of His locks ringleted,
Still on the wine-threshold my face prone I lay.

HAFEZ, awake! Toping no more counts for sin,
Now that our Lord Royal hath put sins away.

W. *Leaf*.

SWIMMING

What time in his hand the bowl he shaketh,
All worth of the beauty-mart he breaketh.

Fish-like in a sea behold me swimming,
Till he with his hook my rescue maketh.

All they that behold his drunken eyes' glance
Cry: 'Call for the reeve, the drunk that taketh.'

When low at his feet I fall complaining,
He raiseth again the heart that acheth.

How blest is the soul that like to HAFEZ
All thirst in the Wine of Heaven slaketh!

W. *Leaf*.

RED ROSE

In quest of the garden of roses At dawn-tide in hope I went,
My brain like the lovelorn bulbul, To solace somedeal with the scent;
And there in the midst of the greensward Mine eyes on a red rose lit,
That shone as a lamp in the darkness, Such light to the meads she lent.
So proudly in youth and beauty She queened it, that all repose
From the bird of the thousand voices She ravished, and heart's content.

The eyes of the wild narcissus Ran over with wistful tears;
And hundreds of scars of passion The heart of the tulip rent.

The lily at her, in chiding, The tongue stretched out, like a sword;.

Th'anemone, blab-like, opened Her mouth in astonishment.

Anon in her hand the flagon, Like lovers of wine; anon,
Like skinkers that fill for topers, The cup on her palm she hent.

Easance, mirth, youth, O Hafez, Enjoy, while they last, like the rose.

The messenger only bound is To carry the message sent.

J. Payne.

FULL FAIR

Fair are rill-bank and willow-foot And songful spright and friend, full fair;

A charmer sweet to mate, a maid Rose-cheeked, our cup to tend, full fair.

O fortune-favoured one, that hast All these and know'st the worth of time,

Hail, for the Fates, indeed, to thee A portion fair extend, full fair!

Bid whoso hath a charmer's love At heart cast rue upon the fire,

For from the evil eye he hath A matter to defend full fair.

Jewels of virgin thought I bind On this my nature's bride; maybe

The cast of Fortune's dice to me An idol fair shall send, full fair.

The nights of union enjoy And take thy share of heart's content;
Heart-kindling for the moonlight is, Ay, and the streamlet's bend full fair.

In her eyes' cup the skinker hath A wine, God wot, that to the wit
Gives drunkenness delectable, And to the very end full fair.

In folly, Hafez, hath life passed: With us unto the wine-house come,
So blithesome fair ones there to thee A business may commend full fair.

J. Payne.

HARVEST

In the green sky I saw the new moon reaping,
And minded was I of my own life's field:
What harvest wilt thou to the sickle yield
When through thy field the moon-shaped knife goes sweeping?

In other fields the sunlit blade is growing,
But still thou sleepest on and takest no heed;
The sun is up, yet idle is thy seed:
Thou sowest not, though all the world is sowing.

Back laughed I at myself: All this thou'rt telling
Of seed-time! The whole harvest of the sky
Love for a single barleycorn can buy,
The Pleiads at two barleycorns are selling.

Thieves of the starry night with plunder shining,
I trust you not, for who was it but you
Stole Kavous' crown, and robbed great Kaikhosrow
Of his king's girdle—thieves, for all your shining!

Once on the starry chess-board stretched out yonder
The sun and moon played chess with her I love,
And, when it came round to her turn to move,
She played her mole —and won— and can you wonder?

Earrings suit better thy small ears than reason,
Yet in their pink shells wear these words to-day:
'Hafez has warned me all must pass away—
Even my beauty is but for a season.'

R. Le Gallienne.

LOVE'S LANGUAGE

Breeze of the morning, at the hour thou knowest,
The way thou knowest, and to her thou knowest,
Of lovely secrets trusty messenger,
I beg thee carry this dispatch for me;
Command I may not: this is but a prayer
Making appeal unto thy courtesy.

Speak thus, when thou upon my errand goest:
'My soul slips from my hand, so weak am I;
Unless thou heal it by the way thou knowest,
Balm of a certain ruby, I must die.'

Say further, sweetheart wind, when thus thou blowest:
'What but thy little girdle of woven gold
Should the firm centre of my hopes enfold?
Thy legendary waist doth it not hold,
And mystic treasures which thou only knowest?'

Say too: 'Thy captive begs that thou bestowest
The boon of thy swift falchion in his heart;
As men for water thirst he to depart
By the most speedy way of death thou knowest.

'I beg thee that to no one else thou showest
These words I send —in such a hidden way
That none but thou may cipher what I say;
Read them in some safe place as best thou knowest.'

When in her heart these words of mine thou sowest
For HAFEZ, speak in any tongue thou knowest;
Turkish and Arabic in love are one—
Love speaks all languages beneath the sun.

R. *Le Gallienne.*

STRIFE

The calm circumference of life
When I would fain have kept,
Time caught me in the tide of strife
And to the centre swept.

Of this fierce glow which Love and You
Within my breast inspire,
The Sun is but a spark that flew
And set the heavens afire!

R. A. *Nicholson.*

THE BELOVED

Mortal never won to view thee,
Yet a thousand lovers woo thee;
Not a nightingale but knows
In the rose-bud sleeps the rose.

Love is where the glory falls
Of thy face: on convent walls
Or on tavern floors the same
Unextinguishable flame.

Where the turban'd anchorite
Chanteth Allah day and night,
Church-bells ring the call to prayer,
And the Cross of Christ is there.

R. A. *Nicholson.*

REVELATION

My soul is the veil of his love,
Mine eye is the glass of his grace.
Not for earth, not for heaven above,
Would I stoop; yet his bounties have bowed
A spirit too proud
For aught to abase.

This temple of awe, where no sin
But only the zephyr comes nigh,
Who am I to adventure within?
Even so: very foul is my skirt.
What then? Will it hurt
The most Pure, the most High?

He passed by the rose in the field,
His colour and perfume she stole.
Oh twice-happy star that revealed
The secret of day and of night–
His face to my sight,
His love to my soul!

R. A. Nicholson

WILD DEER

1

Whither fled, wild deer?
I knew thee well in days gone by
When we were fast friends, thou and I;
Two solitary travellers now,
Bewildered, friendless, I and thou,
We go our separate ways, where fear
Lurks ambushed, front and rear.

Come, let us now inquire
How each is faring; let us gain
(If gain we may, upon this plain
Of trouble vast, where pastures pure
From fear secure
Are not to find) the spirit's far desire.

2

Beloved friends, declare:
What manner of man is there
That shall the lonely heart befriend,
That shall the desolate attend?
Khezr, the heavenly guide,
He of the footfall sanctified,
Perchance he cometh, and shall bring
In purpose deep and mercy wide
An end of all my wayfaring.

3

'Twas little courtesy
That ancient comrade showed to me.
Moslems, in Allah's name I cry!
The pitiless blow he struck me by,
So pitiless, to strike apart
The cords that bound us heart to heart,
To strike as if it were
No love was ever there.

He went; and I that was so gay
To grief convert; was such the way
Brother should act with brother? Yea,
Khezr, the heavenly guide,
He of the footfall sanctified,
Haply the shadow of his gracious wing
Lone soul to lonely soul shall bring.

4

But surely this the season is
When of the bounty that is His
Allah dispenses; for I took
Lately this omen from the Book:
'Leave me not issueless!' the Prophet cried.

It happened on a day one sat beside
The road, a rare bold fellow; when there went
Upon that way a traveller intent
To gain the goal. Gently the other spake:
'What in thy scrip, Sir traveller, dost thou take?
If it be truly grain, come, set thy snare.'
The traveller answered: 'Grain indeed I bear;
But, mark this well, the quarry I would win
Shall be the Phoenix.' 'Certes, then how begin
The quest?' the other asked. 'What sign hast thou
To lead thee to his eyrie? Not till now
Have we discovered any mark to guide
Upon that quest. By what weight fortified
Shall our dire need those scales essay to hold
Wherein the sun hath cast his purse of gold?'

5

Since that cypress tall and straight
Joined the parting camel-train,
By the cypress sit, and wait
Watchful till he come again.
Here, beside the bubbling spring
Where the limpid river runs,
Softly weep, remembering
Those beloved departed ones.
As each pallid ghost appears,
Speak the epic of thy pain,
While the shower of thy tears
Mingles with the summer rain.
And the river at thy feet,
Sadly slow, and full of sighs,
Tributaries new shall meet
From the fountain of thine eyes.

6

Give never the wine-bowl from thy hand,
Nor loose thy grasp on the rose's stem;
'Tis a mad, bad world that the Fates have planned—
Match wit with their every strategem!

Comrades, know each other's worth;
And when ye have this comment lined
Upon the margin of the mind,
Recite the text by heart:
So say the moralists of this earth;
For lo, the archer ambushed waits,
The unerring archer of the Fates,
To strike old friends apart.

7

When I take pen in hand to write
And thus my marshalled thoughts indite,
By the Eternal Pen,
What magic numbers then
Flow from my fingers, what divine
And holy words are mine!
For I have mingled Soul with Mind,
Whereof the issuing seed I have consigned
To music's fruitful earth;
Which compound brings to birth
(As having for its quintessential part
Of poesy the purest art)
Most gladsome mirth.

Then come, I bid thee; let this fragrant scent
Of fairest hope, and soft content,
Bear to thy soul delight eternal:
For verily the musk's sweet blandishment
Was sprinkled from the robe of sprites supernal;
It was not wafted here
From that wild, man-forsaking deer!

A. J. *Arberry*.

Hunting ground, Mirza Aqa Imami, 26×39 cm., end of the 14th cent. A.H.

The General Office of Bonyad Museums

A party, Mirza Aqa Imami, 55×80 cm., middle of the14th cent. A.H.

JAMI

MORNING AIR

How sweet the gale of morning breathes!
    Sweet news of my delight he brings;
News, that the rose will soon approach
    the tuneful bird of night, he brings.
Soon will a thousand parted souls
    be led, his captives, through the sky,
Since tidings, which in every heart
    must ardent flames excite, he brings.
Late near my charmer's flowing robe
    he pass'd, and kiss'd the fragrant hem;
Thence, odour to the rose-bud's veil,
    and jasmine's mantle white, he brings.
Painful is absence, and that pain
    to some base rival oft is ow'd;
Thou know'st, dear maid! when to thine ear
    false tales, contriv'd in spite, he brings.
Why should I trace love's mazy path,
    since destiny my bliss forbids?
Black destiny! my lot is woe,
    to me no ray of light he brings.
In vain a friend his mind disturbs,
    in vain a childish trouble gives,
When sage physician to the couch
    of heart-sick lovelorn wight, he brings.
A roving stranger in thy town,
    no guidance can sad JAMI find,
Till this his name, and rambling lay,
    to thine all-piercing sight he brings.

Sir William Jones.

SOLITUDE

To unfrequented worlds I soaring fly,
Sad is the town without thy cheering eye.
Since thou art gone I've no affection known,
And tho' midst crowds, I seem to stray alone.
No dread of solitude my soul assails,
Where'er I go thy image never fails.
Bound with Love's fetters, a distracted swain,
I seek thee thro' the world, and wear thy chain.
Whether on silk or roses of the mead
I tread; all paths to aught but thee that lead,
O'ergrown with thorns, and set with briars rude,
Retard my love, and all my hopes delude.
I said, alas! my life I freely give;
Depriv'd of thee I've no desire to live.
Some spirit whisper'd patience to my heart,
That e'en to-day for aye I might depart.

S. Weston.

TEARS

Unhous'd, unfriended, solitary, slow,
On Tigris' banks I wander to and fro,
And with my tears that flowing never cease,
The torrent of the rapid stream increase.

S. Weston.

SEQUENCE

1

Thou lookest not upon the prisoner,
Nor visitest the stranger at the gate;
Wilt thou not suffer thy glance on me to err,
That with no other heart is intimate?
Heed not the tales mine enemies relate:
Thou hast no friend than I more friendlier.
My heart's blood filled mine eyelashes of late—
That I am heartless, how canst thou aver?

Yet how shall my lamenting move thy heart
That has no symptom of fidelity?
But, do not drive me from thy door to part,
Though that I suffer is no grief to thee.
Be not ashamed of love's idolatry,
Jami; in this most virtuous thou art.

2

The darling's love has set a table of woe:
Come hither, ye afflicted ones, and eat!
And if she say not yes with kisses sweet,
From that enchantress we are content with no.
The rust of down that on her face doth show
Brightens the eye and heart with light discrete:
Her image hath destroyed my life, and lo,
Her image is my substitute complete.
Now love's distraction plunders on reason's road:
Friends reasonable, guide me on my way!
Yet who shall save me, as I go astray,
Except the one, most high and mighty God?
So much of learning Jami has to say,
Gleaned from the fields where learned men have sowed.

3

Men point their fingers at thy lovely brow
And cry: 'Behold, the Festal Moon is here!'
The promise of a dawn of blessed cheer
Unto thy lovers in thy face doth glow.
The Holy Feast cometh but once a year,
But every day with thee to feast I go,
And of thy cheek so happy a feast I know
As to none other ever did appear.
When thou didst say: 'With grief I'll slay thy soul,'
Yet was that slaying for me a festival.
The tailor Time, measuring thy stature tall,
Cut thee a robe of grace ineffable;
But ah, for Jami this glad carnival,
Not being with thee, is a tide most sorrowful.

4

When from my dust a blood-red flower doth rise,
Upon each leafy branch a bird will sing.
Be not a flame so fiercely ravishing,
Lest my tormented heart dissolve in sighs.
Where'er the echo of a footfall flies
In drunken ecstasy of hope I spring;
When night is loud, and thou art listening,
I am the beggar in thy street that cries.
When from thy lane cometh a messenger,
Swift as my tears I run to ask of thee.
Physician, open thou thy books for me,
The cure of my distemper may be there.
Jami, thine eye must shed full many a tear
Ere ever thy heart its dear desire shall see.

5

For those red lips the hungry soul doth plead
Even as a parrot doth of sugar dream:
Whoever telleth of Salsabil's sweet stream
Yearneth upon that honeyed lip to feed.
Far from that lip, my soul is a wailing reed:
List to the reed and its threnody supreme—
Of lonely waiting it maketh its mournful theme,
Reft of the sugar-lip its dearest need.
He driveth from his side the adversary
And keepeth all his high regard for me;
His roguish eye is a sword ready to slay,
His life-giving lip saveth me in the fray.
What need of a sword, Jami in blood to lay,
When in his glance is cruel sufficiency?

A. J. *Arberry*.

IRAJ

EPITAPH

Know ye, fair folk who dwell on earth
Or shall hereafter come to birth,
That here, with dust upon his eyes,
Iraj, the sweet-tongued minstrel, lies.
In this true lover's tomb interred
A world of love is sepulchred.
Each ringlet fair, each lovely face,
In death, as living, I embrace:
I am the selfsame man ye knew.
That passed his every hour with you.
What if I quit the world's abode?
I wait to join you on the road;
And though this soil my refuge be,
I watch for you unceasingly.
Then sit a moment here, I pray,
And let your footsteps on me stray:
My heart, attentive to your voice,
Within this earth's heart will rejoice.

A. J. Arberry.

MOTHER

They say, when first my mother bore me
She taught me how to rest
My lips against her breast;
Wakeful at night, and leaning o'er me
Cradled in slumber deep,
She taught me how to sleep.

She kissed my mouth to happy laughter,
And in that magic hour
She taught my rose to flower.
One letter, and two letters after,
She taught me week by week,
Until my tongue could speak.

She took my hand in hers, and leading
Me on, with loving talk
She taught me how to walk.
While I have life, be this my pleading:
Since she my being bore,
I'll love her evermore.

A. J. Arberry.

TAVALLALI

MARY

At the mid-hour of twilight, in the time
When from the west the broken moon doth climb
Pale in the sky, silent and proud and white
Mary stands in the black of night.

Waits till the moonbeams, lifting their gleam above
The mountain's battlements, from night's face remove
The shroud of darkness, waits till their lustrous flow
Bathes her limbs in a silver glow.

Now sleeps the garden; the thieving hands of the breeze
Each happy blossom's perfume shamelessly seize;
Tranquil the night is sleeping; but Mary's eyes
Watch the night in the moon-washed skies.

Little by little behind the willow's boughs
The moonbeams thievishly steal, and through the drowse
Of the black night, as Mary seeks them, astir,
Eagerly gaze they, seeking her.

Darkness gathers her skirts, and headlong flees
From the moon's radiance unto the distant trees;
Sweet, sweet is night; the moonlight dewy and deep
Floods the spirit and lulls asleep.

Amidst the garden's happy and whispering hush
Quivers the silken moon in the brook; a thrush
Bursts into song this instant, and from the bough
Carols: 'Mary is bathing now.'

A. J. *Arberry*.

SAD LOVE

Below the ancient plane
That since so long ago,
Head lifted so,
Solitary
Stands in the plain
A lonely tree,
Love, too worn out to weep
For Fate,
Too sad, too desolate,
Love lies asleep.

And now the ravens come
Swooping on crowded wing,
Come clamouring
To their lost tree
That is their home
Where they would be
At eventide, they sweep
In flight
Calling, that through the night
Still they may sleep.

As coming from afar
Heavy and slow of breath
Night entereth;
Winking on high
Each flickering star
Looks down, to spy
What haps on earth. A peace
Profound
And awful reigns; no sound;
Eve's whispers cease.

Anon out of the heart
Of some black, lowering cloud
That caps a proud
Far mountain-head
Quick lightnings dart,
Sudden and red.
From a dark corner bathed
In gloom
A spirit from the tomb
Stirs, shadow-swathed.

Beside the ruined tower
Where once a fortress rose
A flame now glows
The nymph of night
Kindled this hour;
There, by the bright
Fire she is sleeping. Lo,
Around
The gleam a ghost aswound
Sweeps, and shrills woe.

Down from the mountain's brows
A wind, drawn suddenly,
Upon the tree
Rushes unpent
And thrusts its boughs
To the earth, bent.
So, with a twisted limb
The plane
Seizes sad Love amain
And wakens him.

A. J. Arberry.

KHANLARI

NIGHT THE PLUNDERER

Night came to plunder, and with open fist
Seized all that stirred within the hollow vale:
Long since the river was his captive-list,
And you might hear the river's plaintive wail.

The garden's treasure, purple, crimson, white,
All vanished into night's far-plundering hand;
The walnut bough lifted its foot in fright
High o'er the apple branch, and upwards spanned.

Like a black smoke its swirling skirt night drew,
Hastening from the lowland to the hill;
The forest's hands and feet were lost to view,
The concourse of the trees was hushed and still.

'Night! night!' the screech-owl's warning echo leapt,
And a leaf shivered on a willow limb;
Along the earth a wandering straggler crept
Until the thick mint-bushes swallowed him.

Night drew a long, warm sigh, to sleep at last
Reposeful after strife and stress, content:
A poplar and some ancient willows fast
Fled o'er the hillock's brow, incontinent.

A. J. *Arberry*.

ODE

RUDAKI

LAMENT IN OLD AGE

Every tooth, ah me! has crumbled, dropped and fallen in decay!
Tooth it was not, nay say rather, 'twas a brilliant lamp's bright ray;
Each was white and silvery-flashing, pearl and coral in the light,
Glistening like the stars of morning or the raindrop sparkling bright;
Not a one remaineth to me, lost through weakness and decay.
Whose the fault? "Twas surely Saturn's planetary rule,' you say.
No, the fault of Saturn 'twas not, nor the long, long lapse of days;
'What then?' I will answer truly: 'Providence which God displays.'
Ever like to this the world is —all of dust as in the past,
Ball of dust for aye remaineth, long as its great law doth last.
That same thing which once was healing, may become a source of pain;
And the thing that now is painful, healing balm may prove again—
Time, in fact, at the same moment bringeth age where once was youth,
And anon rejuvenateth what was gone in eld, forsooth.
Many a desert waste existeth where was once garden glad;
And a garden glad existeth where was once a desert sad.
Ah, thou moon-faced, musky-tressed one, how canst thou e'er know or deem
What was once thy poor slave's station—how once held in high esteem?
On him now thy curling tresses, coquettish thou dost bestow,
In those days thou didst not see him, when his own rich curls did flow.
Time there was when he in gladness, happy did himself disport,
Pleasure in excess enjoying, though his silver store ran short;

Always bought he in the market, countless-priced above the rest,
Every captive Turki damsel with a round pomegranate breast.
Ah! how many a beauteous maiden, in whose heart love for him reigned,
Came by night as pilgrim to him, and in secret there remained!
Sparkling wine and eyes that ravish, and the face of beauty deep,
High-priced though they might be elsewhere, at my door were ever cheap.
Always happy, never knew I what might be the touch of pain,
And my heart to gladsome music opened like a wide champaign.
Many a heart to silk was softened by the magic of my verse,
Yea, though it were hard as flintstone, anvil-hard, or even worse.
Ever was my keen eye open for a maid's curled tresses long,
Ever alert my ear to listen to the word-wise man of song.
House I had not, wife nor children, no, nor female family ties,
Free from these and unencumbered have I been in every wise.
Rudaki's sad plight in old age, Sage, thou verily dost see;
In those days thou didst not see him as this wretch of low degree.
In those days thou didst not see him when he roved the wide world o'er,
Songs inditing, chatting gaily, with a thousand tales and more.
Time there was when that his verses broadcast through the whole world ran,
Time there was when he all-hailed was, as the bard of Khorasan.
Who had greatness? Who had favour, of all people in the land?
I it was had favour, greatness, from the Saman scions' hand;
Khorasan's own Amir, Nasr, forty thousand dirhams gave,
And a fifth to this was added by the Prince of the Pure and Brave;
From his nobles, widely scattered, came a sixty thousand more;
Those the times when mine was fortune, fortune good in plenteous store.
Now the times have changed—and I, too, changed and altered must succumb,
Bring the beggar's staff here to me; time for staff and scrip has come!

A. V. Williams Jackson.

FARROKHI
THE BRANDING

Since the meadow hides its face in satin shot with greens and blues,
And the mountains wrap their brows in silken veils of seven hues,
Earth is teeming like the musk-pod with aromas rich and rare,
Foliage bright as parrot's plumage doth the graceful willow wear.
Yestere'en the midnight breezes brought the tidings of the spring:
Welcome, O ye northern gales, for this glad promise which ye bring!
Up its sleeve the wind, meseemeth, pounded musk hath stored away,
While the garden fills its lap with shining dolls, as though for play.
On the branches of syringa necklaces of pearls we see,
Ruby earrings of Badakhshan sparkle on the Judas-tree.
Since the branches of the rose-bush carmine cups and beakers bore
Human-like five-fingered hands reach downwards from the sycamore.
Gardens all chameleon-coated, branches with chameleon whorls,
Pearly-lustrous pools around us, clouds above us raining pearls!
On the gleaming plain this coat of many colours doth appear,
Like a robe of honour granted in the court of our Amir.
For our Prince's Camp of Branding stirreth in these joyful days
So that all this age of ours in joyful wonder stands agaze.
Green within the green you see, like skies within the firmament;
Like a fort within a fortress spreads the army tent on tent.
Every tent contains a lover resting in his sweetheart's arms,
Every patch of grass revealeth to a friend a favourite's charms.
Harps are sounding midst the verdure, minstrels sing their lays divine;
Tents resound with clink of glasses as the pages pour the wine.
Kisses, claspings from the lovers; coy reproaches from the fair;
Wine-born slumbers for the sleepers, while the minstrels wake the air.

Branding-fires, like suns ablaze, are kindled at the spacious gate
Leading to the state pavilion of our Prince so fortunate.
Leap the flames like gleaming standards draped with yellow-hued brocade,
Hotter than a young man's temper, yellower than gold assayed.
Branding-tools like coral branches ruby-tinted glow amain
In the fire, as in the ripe pomegranate glows the crimson grain.
Rank on rank of active boys, whose watchful eyes no slumber know;
Steeds which still await the branding, rank on rank and row on row.
On his horse, the river-forder, roams our genial Prince afar,
Ready to his hand the lasso, like a young Isfandiyar.
Like the locks of pretty children see it how it curls and bends,
Yet be sure its hold is stronger than the covenant of friends.
Bú'l-Muzaffar Shah the Just, surrounded by a noble band,
King and conqueror of cities, brave defender of the land.
Serpent-coiled in skilful hands fresh forms his whirling noose doth take,
Like unto the rod of Moses metamorphosed to a snake.
Whosoever hath been captured by that noose and circling line,
On the face and shoulder ever bears the Royal Sign.
But, though on one side he brands, he giveth also rich rewards,
Leads his poets with a bridle, binds his guests as though with cords.

E. G. Browne.

ASADI

NIGHT AND DAY

Hear the fierce dispute and strife which passed between the Night and Day;
'Tis a tale which from the heart will drive all brooding care away.
Thus it chanced, that these disputed as to which stood first in fame,
And between the two were bandied many words of praise and blame.

Hunting ground, Hosain Khataei, 81×120 cm., 1385 A.H., watercolor and gilding on leather

Hunting ground, Mirza Aqa Imami, 83×102 cm.,
middle of the14th cent. A.H., watercolor and gilding on leather

'Surely Night should take precedence over Day,' began the Night,
'Since at first the Lord Eternal out of Darkness called the Light.
Do not those who pray by daylight stand in God's esteem less high
Than do those who in the night-time unto Him lift up their cry?
In the night it was that Moses unto prayer led forth his throng,
And at night-time Lot departed from the land of sin and wrong.
'Twas at night that by Mohammad heaven's orb in twain was cleft,
And at night on his ascent to God the Holy House he left.
Thirty days make up the month, and yet, as God's Qur'an doth tell,
In degree the *Night of Merit* doth a thousand months excel.
Night doth draw a kindly curtain, Day our every fault doth show;
Night conferreth rest and peace, while Day increaseth toil and woe.
In the day are certain seasons when to pray is not allowed,
While of night-long prayer the Prophet and his Church were ever proud.
I'm a King whose throne is earth, whose palace is the vaulted blue,
Captained by the Moon, the stars and planets form my retinue.
Thou with thy blue veil of mourning heaven's face dost hide and mar,
Which through me, like Eram's Garden, glows with many a flower-like star.
By this Moon of mine they count the months of the Arabian year,
And the mark of the Archangel's wing doth on its face appear.
On the visage of the Moon the signs of health one clearly sees,
While apparent on the Sun's face are the symptoms of disease.
Less than thirty days sufficeth for the Moon her course to run,
Such a course as in the year is scarce completed by the Sun.'
When the Day thus long had listened to the Night, its wrath was stirred
'Cease!' it cried, 'for surely never bath a vainer claim been heard!

Heaven's Lord doth give precedence, in the oath which He hath sworn,
Over Night to Day; and darest thou to hold the Day in scorn?
All the fastings of the people are observed and kept by day,
And at day-time to the Ka'ba do the pilgrims wend their way.
'Arafa and 'Ashura, the Friday prayer, the festal glee,
All are proper to the Day, as every thinking mind can see.
From the void of Non-Existence God by day created men,
And 'twill be by day, we know, that all shall rise to life again.
Art thou not a grief to lovers, to the child a terror great,
Of the Devil's power the heart, and on the sick man's heart the weight?
Owls and bats and birds of darkness, ghosts and things of goblin race,
Thieves and burglars, all together witness to the Night's disgrace.
I am born of Heaven's sunshine, thou art of the Pit's dark hole;
I am like the cheerful fire-light, thou art like the dusky coal.
These horizons I adorn by thee are rendered dull and drear;
Leaps the light in human eyes for me, for thee springs forth the tear.
Mine Faith's luminous apparel, Unbelief's dark robe for you;
Mine the raiment of rejoicing, thine the mourner's sable hue.
How canst thou make boast of beauty with thy dusky negro's face?
Naught can make the negro fair, though gifted with a statue's grace.
What avail thy starry hosts and regiments, which headlong fly
When my Sun sets up his standard in the verdant field of sky?
What if in God's Holy Book my title after thine appears?
Doth not God in Scripture mention first the deaf, then him who hears?
Read the verse, "He Death created," where Life holds the second place,
Yet is Life most surely welcomed more than Death in any case.
By thy Moon the months and years in Arab computation run,
But the Persian months and years are still computed by the Sun.
Though the Sun be sallow-faced, 'tis better than the Moon, I ween;
Better is the golden *dinar* than the *dirham's* silver sheen.

From the Sun the Moon derives the light that causeth it to glow;
In allegiance to the Sun it bends its back in homage low.
If the Moon outstrips the Sun, that surely is no wondrous thing:
Wondrous were it if the footman should not run before the King!
Of the five appointed prayers the Night has two, the Day has three;
Thus thy share hath been diminished to be given unto me.
If thou art not yet content with what I urge in this debate,
Choose between us two an umpire just and wise to arbitrate;
Either choose our noble King, in equity without a peer,
Or elect, if you prefer, that Mine of Grace, the Grand Vazir,
Ahmad's son Khalil Abu Nasr, noble, bounteous, filled with zeal,
Crown of rank and state, assurer of his King's and country's weal.'

E. G. Browne.

NASER KHOSROW

MESSAGE

Bear from me to Khorasan, Zephyr, a kindly word,
To its scholars and men of learning, not to the witless herd,
And having faithfully carried the message I bid thee bear,
Bring me news of their doings, and tell me how they fare.
I, who was once as the cypress, now upon Fortune's wheel
Am broken and bent, you may tell them; for thus doth Fortune deal.
Let not her specious promise you to destruction lure:
Ne'er was her covenant faithful; ne'er was her pact secure.

Look at Khorasan only: she is crushed and trodden still
By this one and then by that one, as corn is crushed in the mill.
You boast of your Turkish rulers: remember the power and sway
Of the Zawoli Sultan Mahmoud were greater far in their day.
The Royal House of Farighun before his might did bow,
And abandon the land of Juzjan; but where is Mahmoud now?
'Neath the hoofs of his Turkish squadrons the glory of India lay,
While his elephants proudly trampled the deserts of far Cathay.

And ye, deceived and deluded, before his throne did sing:
'More than a thousand summers be the life of our Lord the King!
Who, on his might relying, an anvil of steel attacks,
Findeth the anvil crumble under his teeth like wax!'
The goal of the best was Zawol, as it seems, but yesterday,
Whither they turned, as the faithful turn to Mecca to pray.
Where is the power and empire of that King who had deemed it meet
If the heavenly Sign of Cancer had served as a stool for his feet?
Alas! Grim Death did sharpen against him tooth and claw,
And his talons are fallen from him, and his teeth devour no more.

Be ever fearful of trouble when all seems fair and clear,
For the easy is soon made grievous by the swift-transforming sphere.
Forth will it drive, remorseless, when it deemeth the time at hand,
The King from his Court and Castle, the lord from his house and land.
Ne'er was exemption granted, since the Spheres began to run,
From the shadow of dark eclipses to the radiant Moon and Sun.
Whate'er seems cheap and humble and low of the things of earth
Reckon it dear and precious, for Time shall lend it worth.
Seek for the mean in all things, nor strive to fulfil your gain,
For the Moon when the full it reacheth is already about to wane.
Though the heady wine of success should all men drug and deceive,
Pass thou by and leave them, as the sober the drunkards leave.
For the sake of the gaudy plumage which the flying peacocks wear,
See how their death is compassed by many a springe and snare!

Thy body to thee is a fetter, and the world a prison-cell:
To reckon as home this prison and chains do you deem it well?
Thy soul is weak in wisdom and naked of works beside:
Seek for the strength of wisdom: thy nakedness strive to hide.

Thy words are the seed; thy soul is the farmer; the world the field
Let the farmer look to the sowing, that the soil may abundance yield.

Yet dost thou not endeavour, now that the Spring is here,
To garner a little loaflet for the Winter which creepeth near.
The only use and profit which life for me doth hold
Is to weave a metrical chaplet of coral and pearls and gold!

E. G. Browne.

ANVARI

THE TEARS OF KHORASAN

O gentle Zephyr! if o'er Samarqand
Some dewy morning thou should'st chance to blow,
Then waft this letter to our monarch's hand,
Wherein KHORASAN tells her tale of woe.
Wherein the words that for the heading stand
Are present danger and destruction nigh;
Wherein the words that are inscribed below
Are grief, and wretchedness, and misery;
On every fold a martyr's blood appears,
From every letter breathes a mourner's sigh;
Its lines are blotted with the orphan's tears,
Its ink the widow's burning anguish dries!
Its bare recital wounds the listener's ears,
Its bare perusal scathes the reader's eyes.
What! is KHORASAN's most unhappy case
Unknown to him in whose domain she lies?
No, for his knowledge doth all things embrace,
Whate'er of good or evil is displayed,
In earth's wide limits or in boundless space.
For such things doubtless was provision made;
And now at length to Iran's succour—now
His conquering armies shall the land invade.

Thou, just as Khosrow, mighty monarch, thou
  In whom the blood of seventy kings doth run!
Thy lineage and the diadem on thy brow,
  These are proud boasts, but surely thou hast none
So proud as this—that to the kings of earth
  Great Sultan Sanjar owned thee for his son!
Avenge, as should a son of noble birth,
  Thy father's wrongs upon this Tartar horde!
If of thy wardship Turan knows no dearth,
  Shall Iran be uncared for by her lord?
Kiyumars, king of good renown and just,
  Great Kasra, swift to punish or reward,
Manuchehr, in his presence so august,
  Afridun, in his majesty and might—
Compared with thee, these were but vilest dust.
  Oh! hear the story which I now recite,
And when thou hearest it compassionate,
  And let thy slaves find favour in thy sight.
Oppressed and humbled by opposing fate,
  To thee, her hope, her glory, and her joy,
KHORASAN pleads in her forlorn estate.
  No soul, thou knowest well, may there enjoy
A moment's safety from the Tartar troop;
  All trace of good from Iran they destroy,
Good men to bad men are compelled to stoop,
  The noble are subjected to the vile,
The priest is pressed to fill the drunkard's stoup.
  No man therein is ever seen to smile,
Save at the blow that brings release—and doom!
  No maiden lives that they do not defile,
Except the maid within her mother's womb!
  In every town the mosque and house of prayer—
To give their horses and their cattle room—
  Is left all roofless, desolate, and bare.
'Prayer for our Tartar rulers' there is none
  In all KHORASAN, it is true—for where,
Where are the preachers and the pulpits gone?
  There mothers, when by the assassin's steel

They see their children murdered one by one,
    Dare not give utterance to the grief they feel.
The freeman, kidnapped by the Tartar chief,
    And sold again, rejoices in the deal;
For change –a change of masters –brings relief.
    Their lawcourts give such fair –God save us! –play
When Muslims litigate with unbelief,
    Not one in fifty ever gains the day.
In Room and Khata, in the very lands
    Where Kafers hold an undisputed sway,
The Muslim on an equal footing stands;
    For Muslim countries is the right reserved
To wrest the right from out the Muslim's hands!
    Oh! thou who never from the right hast swerved,
Release thy country from this load of shame;
    For God's sake –God, whom thy forefathers served,
Who on our coinage hath inscribed thy name,
    Who on thy brow hath placed the regal crown,
And given thee all things, power and wealth and fame!
    For God's sake, who on tyranny doth frown,
For God's sake, hear a sorrowing land's request,
    And put these plundering Tartar ruffians down!
Now is the time to set thy lance in rest,
    Now is the time to draw the avenging blade.
Last year their strongholds did thine arms invest,
    Thou didst bear off, in one successful raid,
Wives, wealth, and children-make a fresh attack,
    And of their very lives shall spoil be made!
Fair Iran rivalled Paradise –Alack!
    Though humbled sorely, she will make a stand
Against the oppressors, and will drive them back,
    If thou but bid her. Thou didst make the land
Like Eden's bowers, while those who on her prey
    Have made her worse than hell's hot sulphurous strand.
If one possesseth in KHORASAN, say
    An ass or mule, he keepeth them by stealth,
Or sells the treasure at what price he may;
    What, pray, shall he do who hath no such wealth?

Oh! pity those who every day and hour
  In fruitless wailing waste their time and health!
Oh! pity those who, craving coarsest flour,
  Whilom despised the daintiest of sweets!
Oh! pity those who, though in dust they cower,
  Whilom in honour held the loftiest seats!
Oh! pity those who lie on felt, in place
  Of sleeping softly in their silken sheets!
Like Alexander, wander o'er the face
  Of earth, and conquer over land and sea,
For Alexander, by the heavenly grace,
  Hath no successor on the earth but thee.
Thine is the purpose —may success be thine!
  Thine is the conflict —victory must be
Of Him who did the universe design!
  Such earthly sovereignty, such power and might,
Are given to thee by warranty divine.
  When thou dost deck thee in thy armour bright,
Thy foeman decks him in his funeral pall;
  Thy foeman calls for quarter and respite,
When thou dost for thy plumèd helmet call.
  Iran should of thy justice have a share;
Look not upon her in her hour of fall
  As though there were not such a country there!
Thou art the sun-KHORASAN ruined lies;
  The sun is ne'er in his regards unfair,
Alike o'er town and ruin doth he rise.
  Thou art the rain-cloud —Iran is a field
Where every green thing withers up and dies;
  Doth not the rain-cloud then its treasures yield
Both on the desert and the flowery mead?
  Thou art a King —a King should be a shield
To strong and weak in every hour of need.
  Iran and Turan both on thee depend,
Shall Turan thrive and Iran ne'er be freed?
  Never, until thou shalt her cause defend
And urge thy charger in the battle's storm,
  Shall crushed KHORASAN once more rise and send

Back to their native wilds this Tartar swarm.
    When shall thy shout of victory reach the skies?
When shall Khorasan's rallying legions form?
    Thou hast a minister in counsels wise,
Learned in the mysteries of the law, and one
    Who over Islam like a sun doth rise,
Who from thy light hath all his greatness won,
    As souls from knowledge —who for thy fair face
Longs as the moon longs for the glorious sun.
    When all our wrongs, our misery and disgrace,
Are written, he, on direst vengeance bent,
    Will couch his spear and gird him for the race.
May Heaven aid him in his good intent,
    That by his counsels he may give thee aid!
His office is as of a prophet sent
    By God to mediate for the things He made.
Oh! free thy nation from this gathering pest,
    And on the day when men's accounts are paid,
That act of thine shall rank thee with the blest.
    Great Sultan Sanjar, who thy childhood trained
(O thou of kingly qualities possessed!)
    So long as o'er Iranian lands he reign'd
Kamal-od Din was ever at his side,
    And still the credit of his name maintained.
Thou saw'st how then his probity was tried;
    Canst thou not now implicitly rely
On whom a monarch like thy sire relied?
Nothing escaped his penetrating eye
    In Persia, whether it were good or bad,
E'en as the sun that, shining in the sky,
    Makes with his rays the whole creation glad,
Such genial influence over Persia's fate
    His guiding care and ruling wisdom had.
He, in the field, in business of the state,
    Right faithful service to thy house hath shown;
And now have we implored him to relate
    Khorasan's wrongs before the imperial throne
Perchance the tale may make a tear-drop start,
    When all our wrongs and miseries are known.

Thou who hast played a faithful sovereign's part,
  Give credence to a faithful Vizier's word;
He has the story, like his prayers, by heart.
  He is our shield, be thou the avenging sword;
He speaks but for the welfare of the land,
  And not to earn advancement or reward.
In many an art thou hast a master's hand,
  But most of all in poesy divine;
If then, mayhap, I should convicted stand
  Of repetition in this verse of mine,
Judge not too harshly of my feeble lay,
  'Twas direst need that did the rhymes entwine.
'Am'ak, the greatest poet of his day,
  This thought appropriate to my theme expressed:
'O Zephyr! waft this blood-stained dust away
  To Ispahan'; and should our sad request
Be in such manner to the king conveyed,
  Khorasan's wrongs may e'en be yet redressed.
Not till the sun hath his last journey made
  Around the sky and rested him for aye;
Not until then be thy dominion stayed—
  And thy petitioners shall ever pray.

E. H. Palmer.

BAHAR

THE MIRACLE OF SPRING

Recall how with frozen fingers December's clouds outspread
Over the fields and uplands a mantle of ice and snow;
Over the buried roses, over a world of dead
Vengeful as any hangman stalked the exultant crow.

But lo, the abiding wonder! Spirit, that never dies,
Surges anew and vital through the upstanding trees.
See, those spear-armed horsemen, the spreading tulips, rise
Over the plains triumphant, hills, yea, and mountains seize.

Behold, the eager lily leaps to delight the eye,
Spurning the bent narcissus crouched in his self-regard.
Deep in the springing corn-shoots the gleaming violets lie;
Bright with a myriad jewels the wheat-swept fields are starred.
Under the nodding willow the poppy lies in blood—
Sudden the blow that smote her, drenched her in crimson flood.
And now, mid the green profusion of wheat, in mingled hue
Note how the lily argent with lily azure glows;
So, when the sky is stippled with scattered rain-clouds through
Here and here betwixt them the vault of heaven shows.

A. J. Arberry.

SHAHRIYAR

NOCTURNE

When I am alone, to dream,
The wild birds of my fancy stream
Swiftly out, and in the bower,
All with poesy a-flower,
Passionately fluttering
Rise, and soar upon the wing;
Till, when they hear a voice afar,
Fleet as a wind they turn and flee
Home to my mind, and are
Safe closeted with me.

Panorama of the white
Lily-fields, and the wind in flight
Stirring the waves; waves that swell
Like the tolling of a bell
Sweeping to the skies, and there
Scatter; smoke upon the air
Spiralling; and a fleecy cloud
That seemed to say the history
Swathed in its sunset shroud
Of thy eternity.

Like a smoke the willow-tree
Suspended; glittered tremulously
The lake's mirror; from the blue
Sky the sudden moon breaks through
Sprinkling all with quicksilver
The green plain; so softly stir
The waters, split by the moon's prow
Sailing, as when within a glass
The sun caught; ah, that now
The caravan must pass!

In her ruby castle close
The queen sleeps afar; but rose-
Cheeked, the lights of poesy
Limpid, and soft melody,
Sprinkle, gushing from the spring-
Watered meadows, showering
Angelic chorus to inspire
With starry countenances; rare
And precious gifts, to fire
True lovers' hearts, they bear.

There a thicket, and beside
A pool a willow, shaking wide
Glossy tresses' silken chain;
Like a naked maiden, fain
Shamefully to hide her face,
Cast into the lake's embrace
An image, as it might appear
She combeth out her tresses free
All in a glass; see, here
She peeps behind the tree.

Now the lantern of the sun
On all sides scatters, and upon
The horizon's mirror streams;
In the woolly clouds it gleams
Flushing fire; the smoke and flame
Intermingle; and the same

Reflected shimmer from the pool
Shivers, and conjures up anew
Images colourful
As hope, as fair to view.

Liquid as a peacock's wing,
The molten rainbow glittering
Is distilled. The spinner sky
From her gaudy reel on high
Many a fine and tangled skein
Twists and turns; a silken chain
Of ocean's gleam, and of the sun
The flaming tresses of her head,
Into a girdle spun
For heaven of magic thread.

Naked sprites celestial
Into the stream, their tresses all
Waving, in the crystal tide
Lapis lazuli they glide,
Coruscating as a gem;
Far off, smiling after them,
The water-maidens, scattering
The pallid stars, with lifted head
And pride of peacock's wing
All noiselessly we tread.

On the shore of that white sea
Like shadows in a radiance we
Sit, and all the dusty night's
Indigo, in the moonlight's
Limpid spring, from breast and cheek
Wash; but presently we seek
These that have fallen in the well
Of night; in the moon's argent stream
We seek them, these that fell,
Dancing in the white gleam.

A. J. *Arberry*.

GOLCHIN

THE CURTAIN FELL

1

the curtain fell ... behind the veil of mystery
moved the beginning of another mummery
the undulations of the brain valley and hill
the chiaroscuro playing of a fantastic will
and thou in the midst of it sweet as a rose's scent
and in thy heart the love of a dew-drop long long spent
and i like a rose without a leaf within that shade
beneath the hail's flailing fists staggering flayed
before thy foot before that little foot of thine
my heart like to a moon lacking for light to shine
a vast black firmament of unfulfilling days
even as a darkened sun gleaming with shadow rays
long long and swiftly speeding the white breakers sweep
over the broad expanses of hope's pathless deep
upon the petal's cheek upon the crocus' lip
broadly the sighing winds in lamentation weep
upon thy heart-ravishing cheek flutters a smile
my heart free and rejoicing stands enchained the while
upon thy lip lurking the kiss of the wolf's caress
thine eye huge and mortally cold and comfortless
and thy hair ah thy flaxen hair twisted and taut
and all about thee ... like the dream of being ... naught

2

there is a hidden secret scrapes at me
chisels my heart to thy love's conformity
within my soul a sphere whither the sun
entered but never in its brightness shone
for there creation's eyelids that dark night
opened and utterly confounded sight

and there thou art but lacking light to see
mine eye shall find no cognizance of thee
yea thou art there like star and wind and cloud
raining and trembling and lamenting loud
but ah mine ear is stopt my sight is blind
thou art so near but oh so far to find
there is a hidden secret scrapes at me
chisels my heart to thy love's conformity
yet how can it behold thy love at all
where the sun's eye is shrouded in a pall
the memory of death and life for truth
empties my heart of all the blood of youth
yet the remembered hope of seeing thee
fulfils me with renewed vitality
is being's meaning then as it would seem
the hope of seeing one enraptured dream

3

a great tree and branchless and leafless it stands
so dry and so parched gripped in death's icy hands
surpassingly foul like the tomb like a bone
so shrivelled as faces of dead men alone
above it the sky and the stars silent swing
below it like blood boils and bubbles the spring
without it all duststrew and dirtspread and stain
within chill and dampness and void and inane
my brain is the root whence the great tree evolves
this forest of lions hyenas and wolves
and this of my thought the dark valley and deep
and this the spread curtain of my waking sleep
and this the tight cottage of secret and prayer
and this the drawn thread of desire far and fair
a great tree it stands yea a tree hugely great
the claws of the lions and wolves lacerate
where spiders and emmets and snakes swarm with me
and hootowls and ravens and ah memory

affection and anger and wonder and fear
and all blood congealed and a dry withered tear
my brain is the root yea it stands in my brain
these temples of war and disaster and pain
this broad clouded sky dark with cumulus sighs
this broad gleaming heaven where black stars arise
this sky broadly lighted by hope's sun and moon
by hope bright deceitful and hope vanished soon

4

there is the road and my weary foot and the narrow shoe i wear
the well and the pit and the winding whirl and the name and shame i bear
mountain there is and vale there is dense thicket and stone and clay
teeth of the lion and the wolf and the throb of the heart's dismay
anguish there is and hopelessness and sting and nettle and thorn
yet ever onward he bears me on and on by whom am i borne
this is my being that bears me and i know not whence it has come
from whom it is and for what it is so fearful and dangersome
what is this in this heart of mine is it passion or poverty
concupiscence or the fingerprint of a dark dim mystery
what oh what is the heart for whom so turbulent does it rave
what is this the fall and rise breath breath of a crimson wave
amid the valleys within my brain these rivulets serpentine
unto what ocean hurrying down stream on these waters of mine

5

dark the cavern ... and the mountain range is high
hand enchained and foot enfettered there am i
in the heaven of my soul the moon and sun
gleam like two black diamonds darkling and dun
see the cold blood of an agonizing lust
trickles dripping from the stars over the dust
mid the blood and earth and tears and clay a part
something quivers momently ah 'tis the heart

The General Office of Bonyad Museums

Woman and the bird, Mirza Aqa Imami, 56×69 cm.,
second half of the14th cent. A.H., watercolor and gilding on paper

The assembly of San'an Sheikh, Hosain Khataei, 110×129 cm., 1381 A.H., watercolor on leather

ah my heart my watch whose fingers ever creep
ah the speeding of my months and years of sleep
and my life is all this agony to tell
the untimely chiming of a lying bell
dark the cavern ... and the mountain range is high
hand and foot enfettered there my heart must lie
naught is there save the hawk's lonely flight to see
hawk with wing and beak and claw of mystery
naught to hear save the loud silence of the soul
the loud power of a god lacking control
o thou god thou child engendered by my thought
o thou child of my sick loneliness begot
o thou god thou death's shrouded and pallid ghost
thou commander of an unprovisioned host
dark the cavern ... and the mountain range is high
there enchained are thou and there my heart and i

A. J. *Arberry.*

DIDACTIC

SANA'I

THE BLIND MEN AND THE ELEPHANT

Not far from Ghur once stood a city tall
Whose denizens were sightless one and all
A certain Sultan once, when passing nigh,
Had pitched his camp upon the plain hard by,
Wherein, to prove his splendour, rank, and state,
Was kept an elephant most huge and great.
Then in the townsmen's minds arose desire
To know the nature of this creature dire.
Blind delegates by blind electorate
Were therefore chosen to investigate
The beast, and each, by feeling trunk or limb,
Strove to acquire an image clear of him.
Thus each conceived a visionary whole,
And to the phantom clung with heart and soul.

When to the city they were come again,
The eager townsmen flocked to them amain.
Each one of them —wrong and misguided all—
Was eager his impressions to recall.
Asked to describe the creature's size and shape,
They spoke, while round about them, all agape,
Stamping impatiently, their comrades swarm
To hear about the monster's shape and form.
Now, for his knowledge each inquiring wight
Must trust to touch, being devoid of sight,
So he who'd only felt the creature's ear,
On being asked: 'How doth its heart appear? '
'Mighty and terrible,' at once replied,
'Like to a carpet, hard and flat and wide!'
Then he who on its trunk had laid his hand
Broke in: 'Nay, nay! I better understand!

'Tis like a water-pipe, I tell you true,
Hollow, yet deadly and destructive too';
While he who'd had but leisure to explore
The sturdy limbs which the great beast upbore,
Exclaimed: 'No, no! To all men be it known
'Tis like a column tapered to a cone!'
Each had but known one part, and no man all;
Hence into deadly error each did fall.
No way to know the All man's heart can find:
Can knowledge e'er accompany the blind?

E. G. *Browne.*

RUMI

THE SONG OF THE REED

Hear, how yon reed in sadly pleasing tales
Departed bliss and present woe bewails!
'With me, from native banks untimely torn,
Love-warbling youths and soft-ey'd virgins mourn.
O! let the heart, by fatal absence rent,
Feel what I sing, and bleed when I lament:
Who roams in exile from his parent bow'r,
Pants to return, and chides each ling'ring hour.
My notes, in circles of the grave and gay,
Have hail'd the rising, cheer'd the closing day:
Each in my fond affections claim'd a part,
But none discern'd the secret of my heart.
What though my strains and sorrows flow combin'd!
Yet ears are slow, and carnal eyes are blind.
Free through each mortal form the spirits roll,
But sight avails not. Can we see the soul?'
Such notes breath'd gently from yon vocal frame:
Breath'd said I? no; 'twas all enliv'ning flame.
'Tis love, that fills the reed with warmth divine;
'Tis love, that sparkles in the racy wine.

Me, plaintive wand'rer from my peerless maid,
The reed has fir'd, and all my soul betray'd.
He gives the bane, and he with balsam cures;
Afflicts, yet soothes; impassions, yet allures.
Delightful pangs his am'rous tales prolong;
And LAILI'S frantick lover lives in song.
Not he, who reasons best, this wisdom knows:
Ears only drink what rapt'rous tongues disclose.
Nor fruitless deem the reed's heart-piercing pain:
See sweetness dropping from the parted cane.
Alternate hope and fear my days divide:
I courted Grief, and Anguish was my bride.
Flow on, sad stream of life! I smile secure:
THOU livest! THOU, the purest of the pure!
Rise, vig'rous youth! be free; be nobly bold:
Shall chains confine you, though they blaze with gold?
Go; to your vase the gather'd main convey:
What were your stores? The pittance of a day!
New plans for wealth your fancies would invent;
Yet shells, to nourish pearls, must lie content.
The man, whose robe love's purple arrows rend
Bids av'rice rest, and toils tumultuous end.
Hail, heav'nly love! true source of endless gains!
Thy balm restores me, and thy skill sustains.
Oh, more than GALEN learn'd, than PLATO wise!
My guide, my law, my joy supreme arise!
Love warms this frigid clay with mystick fire,
And dancing mountains leap with young desire.
Blest is the soul, that swims in seas of love,
And long the life sustain'd by food above.
With forms imperfect can perfection dwell?
Here pause, my song; and thou, vain world, farewell.

Sir William Jones.

THE PARROT OF BAGDAD

In far-famed Bagdad, in a druggist's shop,
There lived a parrot,—such a clever bird,
That passengers in the bazaar would stop
To hear him. He could utter every word
Of the 'First Chapter.' I have even heard
That the Imam was seriously vexed
Because the parrot's reading was preferred
To his own services, on this pretext,
That Polly threw so much more feeling in the text.

One day a cat, intent upon a mouse,
Caused the poor parrot a tremendous fright
By dashing unawares into the house.
Extremely disconcerted at the sight,
Our parrot spreads its wings, and taking flight
Upwards towards the ceiling, straight proposes,
Aloft and out of danger, to alight
Upon a shelf where stood some oil of roses,
Destined for Beys' and Pashas' plutocratic noses.

He gained the shelf, but, in his haste, alas!
Upset the bottles with a dreadful crash.
His master turned, and saw the gilded glass,
With all its precious contents, gone to smash;
And being a man by nature rather rash,
And apt to be by quick impulses led,
He seized his pipe-stem, made a sudden dash
At the offender, struck him on the head,
And stretched him on the ground to all appearance dead.

He was not killed, but from that very day
A change came over the unlucky brute;
His crest and topmost feathers fell away,
Leaving him bald as the proverbial coot.

But worse than that, he had become quite mute;
That pious language for which heretofore
The folks had held him in such high repute—
His quips and jokes, were silenced, and no more
Attracted crowds of buyers round the druggist's door.

Alike in vain the wretched druggist tries
To make him speak by foul means and by fair;
Even a mirror held before his eyes
Elicits nothing but a vacant stare.
When all else failed, the druggist took to prayer,
And then to cursing; but it did no good,
For Heaven refused to meddle in the affair.
'Tis strange that men should act as though they could
Cajole or frighten Heaven into a yielding mood.

At length, when he had given the matter up,
There came an old man in a Dervish cloak,
With head as bare as any china cup;
Whereon the bird, who always liked a joke,
Chuckled aloud, his sulky silence broke
For the first time since the untoward event,
And thus in sympathizing accents spoke,
Though with an air of ill-disguised content:
'Hollo, old boy! have you upset your master's scent?'

He carried his analogy too far,
And so do more than half the world beside;
They say that such things are not or they are,
And on experience alone decide.
Thus the immortal Abdals, who preside
Over the spheres, can be perceived of few,
Yet their existence cannot be denied;
And of two things submitted to their view,
Men still receive the false one and reject the true.

Two insects on the selfsame blossom thrive,
Equal in form and hue and strength of wing,
Yet this one brings home honey to the hive,
While that one carries nothing but a sting.
So from one bank two beds of rushes spring,
Drawing their moisture from the selfsame rill,
Yet, as the months the alternate seasons bring,
The stalks of one kind will with sugar fill,
The other kind will be but hollow rushes still.

Soil, whether rich or poor, is one to see;
Two men may be alike in outward show,
Yet one an angel and a friend may be,
And one a devil and a mortal foe;
Two streams may in the selfsame valley flow,
With equal clearness may their waters run,
But he who tastes of them alone may know
Which is the sweet and which the bitter one;
For naught is what it seems of all things 'neath the sun.

A prophet's miracles, when brought to test,
Will conquer the magician's vain pretence;
And yet alike the claims of either rest
On contravening our experience,
And foiling our imperfect human sense.
Behold, when Israel's freedom is at stake,
Moses throws down his rod in their defence;
Their rods, too, Pharaoh's skilled magicians take,
Nor is the difference seen till his becomes a snake.

See how the tricksy ape will imitate
Each human being he may chance to see,
And fancy, in his self-conceited pate:
'I do this action quite as well as he.'
Thus does the sinner oft-times bend the knee,
And in the mosque prefer his sad complaint,
Till in his own eyes he appears to be
No whit less pious than the humble Saint—
Ay! and the world believes his sanctimonious feint.

You call him saint, and he is well content
To be a hardened sinner all the same;
But call him sinner, he will straight resent
The insult, and repudiate the name,
As though 'twere in the word that lay the shame,
And not in him to whom the name applies.
The senseless pitcher should not bear the blame
When in the well itself the foulness lies—
But man still seeks to cheat his own and others' eyes.

I saw a man who laid him down to sleep
Beside a fire one cold and wintry night,
When lo! a burning cinder chanced to leap
Out of the hearth and on his lips alight;
Whereat he started up in sudden fright,
And spat it out, and roared aloud with pain.
Without perceiving them, that luckless wight
Had swallowed cinders o'er and o'er again,
But the first one that burnt him made its presence plain.

To save the body from what harms or kills,
Wise Providence this sense of pain employs;
So, too, the spirit's various griefs and ills
May prove at last a stepping-stone to joys.
In earthly pain this hope the sufferer buoys,
That skilful leeches make the body whole;
But when some overpow'ring grief destroys
Our peace, we fly to Him who heals the soul—
Who holds both life and death in His supreme control.

Physicians mend whate'er has gone amiss,
To give sick men relief from present woe:
He overturns the crumbling edifice
That He may build it up again —as though
A man his dwelling-place might overthrow,
And find a treasure where the cottage stood
With which to build a palace —even so
To cleanse the river-bed you dam the flood—
To heal the wound you pare the flesh that taints the blood.

But how shall we define the Infinite?
How shall we fix each fresh and varying phase
That flits for aye across our baffled sight,
And makes us faint and giddy as we gaze?
Yet with his call the fowler oft essays
To bring the errant hawk within his reach;
So, when men wander in life's devious ways,
The Dervish too may utter human speech,
And in mere mortal words immortal truths may teach.

Ye who would search into the truth, beware
Of false instructors, who assume the name
Of Dervish, and the woollen garment wear
Only to hide their inward sin and shame,
Like false Museilima, who dared to claim
The honours due to Ahmad's self alone,
Till in God's time the retribution came.
Good wine and bad are by their perfume known,
And only in results are truth and falsehood shown.

E. H. Palmer.

THE ARTISTS

Example seekest of science springing in the heart?
This contest heed of Chinaman and Roman's art.
The Chinese urged they had the greater painter's skill.
The Romans pleaded they of art the throne did fill.
The sovereign heard them both; decreed a contest fair;
Results the palm should give the worthiest of the pair.
The parties twain a wordy war waged in debate;
The Romans' show of science did predominate.
The Chinamen then asked to have a house assigned
For their especial use; and one for Rome designed;
Th' allotted houses stood on either side one street;
In one the Chinese, one the Roman, artists meet.
The Chinese asked a hundred paints for their art's use;
The sovereign his resources would not them refuse.

Each morning from the treasury rich colours' store
Was served out to the Chinese till they asked no more.
The Romans argued: 'Colour or design is vain;
We simply have to banish soil and filth amain.'
They closed their gate. To burnish then they set themselves;
As heaven's vault, simplicity filled all their shelves.
Vast difference there is 'twixt colours and not one.
The colours are as clouds; simplicity's the moon.
Whatever tinge you see embellishing the clouds,
You know comes from the sun, the moon, or stars in crowds.
At length the Chinamen their task had quite fulfilled.
With joy intense their hearts did beat, their bosoms thrilled.
The sovereign came, inspected all their rich designs,
And lost his heart with wonder at their talents' signs.
He then passed to the Romans, that his eyes might see.
The curtains were withdrawn, to show whate'er might be.
The Chinese paintings all, their whole designs in full,
Reflected truly were on that high-burnished wall.
Whatever was depicted by the Chinese art
Was reproduced by mirrors, perfect every part.

The Romans are our mystics—know, my worthy friend;
No art, no learning; study, none—but gain their end.
They polish well their bosoms, burnish bright their hearts,
Remove all stain of lust, of self, pride, hate's deep smarts.
That mirror's purity prefigures their hearts' trust;
With endless images' reflection it incrust.

Sir James Redhouse.

REMEMBERED MUSIC

'Tis said, the pipe and lute that charm our ears
Derive their melody from rolling spheres;
But Faith, o'erpassing speculation's bound,
Can see what sweetens every jangled sound.

We, who are parts of Adam, heard with him
The song of angels and of seraphim.
Our memory, though dull and sad, retains
Some echo still of those unearthly strains.

Oh, music is the meat of all who love,
Music uplifts the soul to realms above.
The ashes glow, the latent fires increase:
We listen and are fed with joy and peace.

R. A. Nicholson.

THE SPIRIT OF THE SAINTS

There is a Water that flows down from Heaven
To cleanse the world of sin by grace Divine.
At last, its whole stock spent, its virtue gone,
Dark with pollution not its own, it speeds
Back to the Fountain of all purities;
Whence, freshly bathed, earthward it sweeps again,
Trailing a robe of glory bright and pure.

This Water is the Spirit of the Saints,
Which ever sheds, until itself is beggared,
God's balm on the sick soul; and then returns
To Him who made the purest light of Heaven.

R. A. Nicholson.

THE TRUE SUFI

What makes the Sufi? Purity of heart;
Not the patched mantle and the lust perverse
Of those vile earth-bound men who steal his name.
He in all dregs discerns the essence pure:
In hardship ease, in tribulation joy.
The phantom sentries, who with batons drawn
Guard Beauty's palace-gate and curtained bower,
Give way before him, unafraid he passes,
And showing the King's arrow, enters in.

R. A. Nicholson.

REALITY AND APPEARANCE

'Tis light makes colour visible: at night
Red, green, and russet vanish from thy sight.
So to thee light by darkness is made known:
All hid things by their contraries are shown.
Since God hath none, He, seeing all, denies
Himself eternally to mortal eyes.
From the dark jungle as a tiger bright,
Form from the viewless Spirit leaps to light.
When waves of thought from Wisdom's Sea profound
Arose, they clad themselves in speech and sound.
The lovely forms a fleeting sparkle gave,
Then fell and mingled with the falling wave.
So perish all things fair, to readorn
The Beauteous One whence all fair things were born.

R. A. Nicholson.

THE UNSEEN POWER

We are the flute, our music is all Thine;
We are the mountains echoing only Thee;
Pieces of chess Thou marshallest in line
And movest to defeat or victory;
Lions emblazoned high on flags unfurled—
Thy wind invisible sweeps us through the world.

R. A. Nicholson.

THE PROGRESS OF MAN

First he appeared in the realm inanimate;
Thence came into the world of plants and lived
The plant-life many a year, nor called to mind
What he had been; then took the onward way
To animal existence, and once more
Remembers naught of that life vegetive,
Save when he feels himself moved with desire
Towards it in the season of sweet flowers,
As babes that seek the breast and know not why.

Again the wise Creator whom thou knowest
Uplifted him from animality
To Man's estate; and so from realm to realm
Advancing, he became intelligent,
Cunning and keen of wit, as he is now.
No memory of his past abides with him,
And from his present soul he shall be changed.
Though he is fallen asleep, God will not leave him
In this forgetfulness. Awakened, he
Will laugh to think what troublous dreams he had,
And wonder how his happy state of being
He could forget, and not perceive that all
Those pains and sorrows were the effect of sleep
And guile and vain illusion. So this world
Seems lasting, though 'tis but the sleeper's dream;
Who, when the appointed Day shall dawn, escapes
From dark imaginings that haunted him,
And turns with laughter on his phantom griefs
When he beholds his everlasting home.

R. A. Nicholson.

SA'DI

COMPASSION

Crush not yon ant, who stores the golden grain:
He lives with pleasure, and will die with pain:
Learn from him rather to secure the spoil
Of patient cares and persevering toil.

Sir William Jones.

BENEFICENCE

Who for the hungry spreads a bounteous board,
Of worldly fame lays up a gen'rous hoard.
In active goodness unremitting prove,
And imitate below your God above.

S. Weston.

The assembly of Yusof and Zoleikha, unsigned, 92×157cm., first half of the 13th cent. A.H.

Danseuse, unsigned, 87×143 cm., first half of the 13th cent. A.H.

DIVINE PROVIDENCE

Behold yon azure dome, the sapphire sky,
Rear in unpillar'd might its canopy!
That vast pavilion gemm'd with world of light
Whose circling glories boast a boundless flight
And as they roll, survey man's chequered state,
And scan the destinies of mortal fate.
Here the poor sentry takes his lonely stand,
There throned in state, a monarch rules a land;
Here in the various grades of life, behold
Beggars for justice of th' imperial gold.
Here one in bootless toil breaks down his health,
There, whose vast treasury o'erflows with wealth;
Here on a mat, reclin'd a harass'd frame,
There on a throne, who boasts the regal name.
Behold in clothing vile some take their stand,
While glow in silk the magnates of the land;
This in the wretchedness of want is found–
To that exhaustless treasuries abound.
This, unsuccessful, blames his hapless fate,
That gains his heart's desire, with hope elate.
One vigour braced–one breathes the helpless sigh;
One grey in years, and one in infancy.
One in religion, one in crime we meet–
One how'd in prayer, one rob'd in dark deceit.
This, wont to bless us; that, too fiercely wrong;
This meekly bows; that dares the battle throng;
This, Lord of dignity, an empire's throne;
That, in sin's bondage, heaves the hopeless groan;
Here is enjoyment; there, imbitter'd pain;
Here droops distress-there soars unbounded gain.
One, in the flow'ry garden of repose,
Another, constant mate of countless woes;
This man with riches' increase swells his store;
That scarce can rear a famish'd offspring poor.
See here, the lamp of gladness beaming bright;
There sorrow turns the fairest day to night!

Here, crowned brows —there, claim'd the tribute just;
This rears his head; that prostrates in the dust.
Here gladness reigns supreme, and there is grief;
Here boasts prosperity; there, needs relief;
These, smiling as the rose from pleasures glow;
Those, spirit wounded, deepest sorrows show.
One breathes his soul in prayer and praise sublime,
Another ends a hardened life in crime.
By day and night, this reads the sacred book;
That, drugg'd by wine, sleeps in yon tavern nook.
One as a pillar in God's temple stands:
Another joins the caffer's faithless bands.
One blest with deeds of faith and charity!
Another whelm'd in seas of infamy.
One prudent, wise, and polish'd here we find,
Another senseless, and of brutish mind;
Here the bold hero dares the mortal strife,
There flies the coward trembling for his life;
These, at the threshold of the living God;
Those, throng the infidels' abandoned road.

E. Pocock.

GUARDIANS

Kings are but guardians who the poor should keep,
Though this world's goods wait on their diadem.
Not for the shepherd's welfare are the sheep;
The shepherd, rather, is for pasturing them.
To-day thou markest one flushed with success,
Another sick with struggles against fate;
Pause but a little while, the earth shall press
His brain that did such plans erst meditate.
Lost is the difference of King and slave
At the approach of destiny's decree;
Should one upturn the ashes of the grave,
Could he discern 'twixt wealth and poverty?

E. B. Eastwick.

JESUS AND THE SINNER

Historians say that in the ancient days,
When Jesus walked on earth (to Him be praise!)
There lived a man so bad, so sunk in sin,
That even Satan was ashamed of him;
The Book contained his name so many times,
No room was left to enter all his crimes.
Perished his tree of life, and bore no fruit,
A stupid, cruel, drunken, swinish brute.
Hard by there dwelt a holy devotee,
Known far and wide for strictest piety;
Each was the marvel of the time and place,
The first of wickedness and this of grace.
Jesus (to Him be praise!) I've heard one day
Forth from the desert came and passed that way;
Th' recluse, descending from his casement high,
Fell at His feet with proud humility;
The lost one gazed with wonder at the sight
Like moth bewildered by the candle's light;
Surely one gentle touch had reached his heart,
From Him who came to take the sinner's part!
Shrinking with shame, his conscience stricken sore,
As shrinks a beggar at a rich man's door,
Tears of repentance rolling down his face,
For days and nights polluted with disgrace,
With fear and hope, God's mercy to invoke,
In earnest prayer, with bated breath be spoke:
'My precious life I've wasted day by day,
My opportunities I've thrown away;
In vice and wickedness surpassed by none,
No single act of goodness have I done;
Would that like me no mortal e'er might be,
Better by far to die than live like me!
He who in childhood dies is free from blame,
Old age comes not to bow his head with shame
Forgive my sins, Creator of the world,
Lest I to blackest depths of hell be hurled.'

On that side, lo! the aged sinner cries,
Not daring heavenward to lift his eyes,
Repentant, weeping, sunk in deep despair:
'Help of the helpless! hear, oh! hear my prayer.'
On this, the devotee puffed up with pride,
With visage sour from far the sinner eyed:
'What brings this ill-starred wretch towards this place,
Dares he to think himself of man's high race?
Headlong to fire eternal he has fallen,
His life to lust's foul whirlwind he has given,
His sin-stained soul what good can show that he
Messiah's company should share with me!
I loathe his hateful countenance, and dread
Lest sin's infection to my bosom spread;
In that great day, when all must present be,
O God! I pray Thee raise him not with me.'
From the all-glorious God a message came
To Jesus (ever blessed be His name!):
'The ignorant and learned both are saved,
Both I accept since both to me have prayed;
The lost one, humbled, with repentant tears
Has cried to me, his cry has reached my ears;
Who helpless lowly seeks, and doth not doubt
The mercy seat, shall never be cast out;
His many wicked deeds I have forgiven,
My boundless mercy bringeth him to heaven;
And should the devotee on that great day
Think it disgrace in heaven with him to stay,
Tell him, Beware! they take thee not to hell
And him to paradise with God to dwell.'

The sinner's bleeding heart in anguish sighs,
The saint upon his piety relies,
Doth he not know that God resisteth pride,
But takes the low in spirit to His side?
Whose heart is vile, but outside fair to see,
For him hell's gates yawn wide, he wants no key,

Humility in His sight is more meet
Than strict religious forms and self-conceit;
Thy self-esteem but proves how bad thou art,
For egotism with God can have no part;
Boast not thyself—however swift his pace,
Not every skilful rider wins the race.
Wise men have left for all this saying true,
And Sa'di in this tale remindeth you,
The sinner penitent hath less to fear
Than he whose piety is not sincere.

W. C. *Mackinnon.*

THE GOOD WIFE

A wife who is charming, obedient, and chaste,
Makes a king of the man knowing poverty's taste.
Go! and boast by the beat of five drums at your gate,
That you have by your side an agreeable mate!
If, by day, sorrow trouble you, be not distressed!
When, by night, a grief-soother reclines on your breast!
When a man's house is thriving, his wife friendly too,
Towards him is directed God's merciful view.
When a lovely-faced woman is modest and nice,
Her husband on seeing her tastes paradise.
The man in this world his heart's longing has found,
Whose wife and himself are in harmony bound.
If choice in her language and chaste in her ways,
On her beauty or ugliness fix not your gaze!
For the heart by an amiable wife's more impressed,
Than by one of great personal beauty possessed;
A sociable nature is hostile to strife,
And covers a number of faults in a wife.
She vinegar sips like liqueur from her spouse,
And eats not her sweetmeats with vinegar brows.
A demon-faced wife, if good-natured withal,
From a bad-tempered, pretty one bears off the ball.
An agreeable wife is a joy to the heart,
But, O God! from a wicked one keep me apart!

As a parrot shut up with a crow shows its rage,
And deems it a boon to escape from the cage;
So, to wander about on the Earth, turn your face!
If you do not, your heart upon helplessness place!
In the magistrate's jail better captive to be,
Than a face, full of frowns, in your dwelling to see.
A journey is *'Eid* to the head of the house,
Who has in his home a malevolent spouse.
The door of delight on that mansion shut to!
Whence issues with shrillness the voice of a shrew!
The woman addicted to gadding, chastise!
If you don't, sit at home like a wife! I advise.
If a wife disregard what her husband should say,
In her breeches of stibial hue, him array!
When a woman is foolish and false to your bed,
To misfortune, and not to a wife, you are wed.
When a man in a measure of barley will cheat,
You may wash your hands clear of the store of his wheat.
The Lord had the good of that servant in view,
When he made his wife's heart and her hands to him true.
When a woman has smiled in the face of strange men,
Bid her husband not boast of his manhood again!
When an impudent wife dips her hand in disgrace,
Go! and tell her to scratch her lord's cuckoldy face!
May the eyes of a wife to all strangers be blind!
When she strays from her home —to the grave be consigned!
When you find that a wife is on fickleness bent,
With wisdom and reasoning, rest not content!
Fly away from her bosom! much better to face
A crocodile's mouth, than to live in disgrace.
To conceal a wife's face from a stranger, you need;
What are husband and wife, if she fails to give heed?
A fine, buxom wife is a trouble and charge;
A wife who is ugly and cross, set at large!
How well this one saying two people expressed,
Whose minds at the hands of their wives were distressed!
One remarked: 'May no man to a vixen be bound!'
Said the other: 'On Earth may no women be found!'

Oh friend! take a bride ev'ry spring that ensues!
For a past season's almanac no one will use.
Better barefooted walk than in tight shoes to roam;
Better travel's misfortune than fighting at home.
Some wives are tyrannical, headstrong, and bold,
But are pleased when they share your embrace, I am told.
Oh *Sa'di*! go to! do not jeer at his life!
When you see that a man is henpecked by his wife.
You, too, are oppressed and her load you abide,
If once you invite her to come to your side!

G. S. Davie.

PRUDENCE

When strong and rich the wicked ones you see,
'Tis good to live resigned, and let them be:
Not having nails to tear away their eyes,
The least of fighting is the most of wise:
Who grapples with an arm of iron breaks
His own wrist —were it silver. Prudence makes
The cautious wait, till Fate their strength constrains,
Then—to the joy of all—dash out their brains.

Sir Edwin Arnold.

THE DERVISH

When the heart wanders, seeking endless change,
And from its own safe solitude doth range,
Not peace it finds, nor any virtue more;
But though a man had merchandise in store
And rank and wealth and lands, his heart being still,
He may live Allah's Dervish, if he will.

Sir Edwin Arnold.

FORGIVENESS

A great stream grows not muddy by one stone,
A Darweesh vexed is like a puddle blown;
If wrong be done, thine injurers forgive,
By pardoning them thyself may'st pardoned live!
Ah, brothers! since the last day brings to dust,
Be dust and ashes now, as then we must.

Sir Edwin Arnold.

EQBAL

COMMUNITY

Upon what manner man is bound to man:
That tale's a thread, the end whereof is lost
Beyond unravelling. We can descry
The Individual within the Mass,
And we can pluck him as a flower is plucked
Out of the garden. All his nature is
Entranced with individuality,
Yet only in Society he finds
Security and preservation. On
The road of life, the furnace of life's fire,
That roaring battle-field, sets him aflame.
Men grow habituated each to each,
Like jewels threaded on a single cord;
Succour each other in the war of life
In mutual bond, like workmen bent upon
A common task. Through such polarity
The constellations congregate, each star
In several attraction keeping each
Poised firmly and unshaken. Caravans
May pitch their tents on mountain or on hill,
Broad meadow, fringe of desert, sandy mound.
Yet slack and lifeless hangs the warp and woof
Of the Group's labour, unresolved the bud

Of its deep meditation, still unplayed
The flickering levin of its instrument,
Its music hushed within its muted strings,
Unsmitten by the pounding of the quest,
The plectrum of desire; disordered still
Its new-born concourse, and so thin its wine
As to be blotted up with cotton flock;
New-sprung the verdure of its soil, and cold
The blood in its vine's veins; a habitat
Of demons and of fairy sprites its thoughts,
So that it leaps in terror from the shapes
Conjured by its own surmise; shrunk the scope
Of its crude life, its narrow thoughts confined
Beneath the rim of its constricting roof;
Fear for its life the meagre stock-in-trade
Of its constituent elements; its heart
Trembling before the whistle of the wind;
Its spirit shies away from arduous toil,
Little disposed to pluck at Nature's skirt,
But whatsoever springs of its own self
Or falls from heaven, that it gathers up.
Till God discovers a man pure of heart
In His good time, who in a single word
A volume shall rehearse; a minstrel he
Whose piercing music gives new life to dust.
Through him the unsubstantial atom glows
Radiant with life, the meanest merchandise
Takes on new worth. Out of his single breath
Two hundred bodies quicken; with one glass
He livens an assembly. His bright glance
Slays, but forthwith his single uttered word
Bestows new life, that so Duality
Expiring, Unity may come to birth.
His thread, whose end is knotted to the skies,
Weaves all together life's dissevered parts.
Revealing a new vista to the gaze,
He can convert broad desert and bare vale
Into a garden. At his fiery breath

A people leap like rue upon a fire
In sudden tumult, in their heart one spark
Caught from his kindling, and their sullen clay
Breaks instantly aflame.   Where'er he treads
The earth receiving vision, every mote
May wink the eye at Moses' Sinai.
The naked understanding he adorns,
With wealth abundant fills its indigence,
Fans with his skirts its embers, purifies
Its gold of every particle of dross.
He strikes the shackles from the fettered slave,
Redeems him from his masters, and declares:
'No other's slave thou art, nor any less
Than those mute idols.'   So unto one goal
Drawing each on, he circumscribes the feet
Of all within the circle of one Law,
Reschools them in God's wondrous Unity,
And teaches them the habit and the use
Of self-surrender to the Will Divine.

A. J. Arberry.

BAHAR

RANDOM THOUGHTS

Above the surface of this low, mean sphere,
Below the heavens' high, enamelled bowl,
None, small or great, lives in contentment here:
Shall I be meanly satisfied in soul?
Deep have I plunged in every subtlety,
Far to the frontier of life's secrets fared:
Being? 'Tis but a dim horizon, we
A point of doubt that on its rim appeared.
Save for that one small, glittering point of doubt
No lustres on that dark horizon rise.
I loved all truths, and yearned to find each out,
But, truly, all was fantasy and lies.

Joy, sorrow, foul and lovely, worst and best,
Are naught but fantasies to my survey:
Dawn's glad effulgence gleams not in my breast,
Nor the last lustre of departing day.
All rebel thought, uprooted from my mind,
Drowns in the whirlpool of a mighty ease,
As when a ship unmasted to the wind
Of fortune yields, and tosses on its seas.

Creation from the start was shaped to be
By nature subject to two monstrous laws:
First, to the influence of heredity,
Next, faculty acquired, a second cause.
If from my ancestors derives my soul,
What in God's name am I, the unfortunate?
If mind and spirit are of my control,
Why shall heredity my doom dictate?
One forbear was a saint and mystic high,
And one an officer and governor;
My father was a poet; therefore I
Should be a poet, saint, and warrior.
My grandfather a merchant was, and so
My father urged me to engage in trade;
Yet all his upbringing was doomed to go
To waste; more toss upon my soul was laid.
No auditor am I, ascetic none,
Merchant nor courtier, officer nor wit;
Curious of all things, but not skilled in one,
Learned in each trade, yet ignorant of it.
Hard as a rock, and heaven's jealous zone
Each instant looses arrows at my heart,
As if I were a red mark on a stone
Set up, fair target for some archer's art.

A. J. Arberry.

PARVIN

MAN AND WIFE

Know'st thou what task the man's may be
And what the wife's, philosopher?
The one a ship is, sailing free;
The other is the mariner.

Then let the captain but be wise,
And let his ship be firm, not frail,
What need they fear, though billows rise
And storm and whirlpool them assail?

For in the evil day of stress
When tossed on fate's tempestuous sea,
Their purpose being singleness,
Both will avert calamity.

Ever the daughter of to-day
Becomes the mother of the morn;
'Tis hers, to set on greatness' way
The sons that of her flesh are born.

A. J. Arberry.

YASIMI

SOCRATES' HOUSE

Socrates, the philosopher wise,
Built him a house of a modest size.
Forthwith about him on every side
People shouted, and people cried;
Each of them had a fault to tell
Of the house he had builded up so well.
This one said: 'It will never do;
It's small and poky, and all askew.'

Another murmured: 'Oh, tut-tut!
So mean and miserable a hut
Scarce beseems, if you want my view,
A man so considerable as you.'
'Well, dear me!' a third broke out,
'A hovel like that? Without a doubt
The great professor we all revere
Can never consent to living here!'
Everyone that his friend was named
All with a single voice exclaimed:
'You can hardly call this a residence
Appropriate to your eminence!
It is so wretched and so small,
One cannot move in it at all;
It is so narrow and so tight
One cannot budge to left or right.'
As the philosopher heard them cry
He laughed aloud, and made reply:
'Friends, you do wrong to criticize;
I cannot call your counsel wise.
Though my small cabin is little worth,
It's everything I require on earth;
All I pray is, that it may be
Filled with friends who are true to me.'

A. J. Arberry.

KHANLARI

THE EAGLE

Sorrowful grew the eagle's spirit and heart
When he beheld the season of youth depart
Far, far away; when he perceived his turn
Was nigh to end, the sun's last radiance burn
The roof-edge of his life. He knew at last
He must capitulate, and forget the past,

And take another road, to another land.
Yet he desired to win into his hand
Some remedy for the inevitable,
To find some elixir rare and wonderful
To ease his mortal sickness. At dawn's light
He rose upon his task, and winged his flight
To heaven upon the swift-paced wind in sweep
Sublime. Far off below, a flock of sheep
That sought to pasture in some verdant plain,
Suddenly startled, bleated, and sprang amain.
The fearful shepherd, anxious at heart, gave chase
Thinking upon his new-born lamb, his pace
Quickening as he ran. A partridge hung
Poised on a bramble. An adder with flicking tongue
Slid smoothly to its hole. A stag stood still
Staring, then swiftly leapt away to the hill
Dragging a trail of dust. But the hunter's heart
Was set on another purpose; he let depart
Free and untroubled his prey. To find a cure
For death is no contemptible task, for sure;
The soul of the living is not wearied so soon
Of life. Every day, and long before the noon,
He might take his prey. To-day a different quest
Than easy prey the hunter's heart possessed.

It chanced that on the margin of the plain
A raven had its nest—hideous, profane,
Of ill report, struck oftentimes by stones
Hurled from small children's hands, yet he kept his bones
Somehow together years past reckoning,
Battened on every foul and horrid thing,
His belly stuffed with corrupting carrion.
The eagle espied him as he perched upon
His twig, and stooping down from heaven high
Addressed him thus: 'O'er much thou hast suffered by
Our unjust persecutions; yet to-day
I would have business with thee, if I may.

There is a problem, which if thou canst find
The solving of, whatever thou hast in mind
To ask of me, I will be pleased to give.'
'Grant me the favour but thy slave to live,'
The raven answered. 'So long as I draw breath
I am thy well-wisher, even unto death,
And little enough is life to yield to thee.
What is thy will? I await obediently
Being ashamed to speak of a thing so small
And inconsiderable as life, since all
My happiness is on thy will to wait.'
All this the raven spoke; but intimate
Within his heart far other words he said.
'Surely 'tis dire necessity doth persuade
This erstwhile tyrant, sinewy till to-day,
To humble himself so meanly, to beg and pray!
Nay, but when sudden anger his heart shall drive
I must be wary, to save my soul alive.
When friendship lacks foundations, it is not wise
From common prudence to avert the eyes.'
So in his heart resolving, he arose
And flapped his wings; further a little he chose
A spot for nesting. Sadly and mournfully
The eagle spoke. 'Alas, what is life to me
But a bubble upon the waters? Though it be true
Ever on sudden and soaring pinion I flew,
The flight of time is fleeter and faster still.
Swiftly I ever passed over plain and hill,
Ah, but as swiftly the days passed over my head.
Nor is the heart sated of life; yet life's sped,
And death cometh on, and counsel is all denied.
Behold my royal pinion, my pomp and pride:
Why is my tale of days so numbered and few?
Thou with thy wings unwieldy, thy stature askew,
By what device didst thou find such length of days?
A black-polled raven there was, that a hundred ways
My father's father, when he was upon the chase,
Escaped with infinite cunning; bird of no grace,

Yet he fled his talons. In turn my father chased
But failed to fold hands on thee, ere he must haste
Unto his home eternal. Even now
As he saw thee perch upon thy favourite bough,
Drawing his ultimate breath, in vain regret
He said to me: "Yon filthy raven is yet
The same that he ever was!" Now my life goes
In turn to plunder; yet no single rose
Of thy hundred roses has blossomed. Oh tell me,
What is the source of thy great longevity?
A secret is hidden here: do thou unfold
This secret.' 'If to this purpose thou wilt hold,'
The raven answered, 'take me a faithful vow
To receive my words. What cause of complaint hast thou
And thy like, if your days are few? The fault is yours,
None other's. All the day your squadron soars
In highest heaven; never ye condescend
To fly more humbly. Well, and what in the end
Profits your soaring? Six hundred years and more
Fashioned my sire to counsel and learned lore,
And oft he said: "The winds that freely roam
Exert enormous influence on the dome
Of upper ether; those that gently blow
Above the dust work never hurt or woe
On soul or body. A little loftier rise
Above the earth, and mischief every wise
The wind will do thee; till, when thou art come
To the skies' zenith, condominium
Of death and ruin there holds patent sway."
Therefore these many years we have turned away
Our faces from the heights; the raven's heart
Inclines towards the depths, and so his part
Is length of years. More, 'tis the property
Of carrion, that they who eat it be
Exceedingly long-lived; foul carrion
Is the best cure, and easiest is won
Thereby relief from all thy griefs and fears.
Henceforward seek not to ascend the spheres,

A woman playing dulcimer, unsigned, 87×143 cm., first half of the 13th cent. A.H.

A young lady in the flower garden, Hosain Behzad, 17×24 cm., 1340 A.H.

Look not to find thy victuals in the skies;
I, who do know a hundred subtleties
And pick my way through every alley and yard,
At the back of a certain garden a house I guard
Secretly for my cache; my table is there
Spread with all manner of eatables sweet and rare.'

The place that the raven hinted of to his friend
Was naught but a dunghill down at the garden's end;
The horrible stench thereof spread far and wide;
There flies would cluster, and hornets ever abide,
A plaguy spot, disgusting to soul and heart,
Scorching the eyes with a terrible blinding smart.
There the two wanderers rested, their journey made,
And there the raven, beholding his table laid,
Exclaimed: 'A board so richly and rarely spread
Is meet for a guest so distinguished to be fed
Therefrom; I give thanks that no poor pauper am I,
Nor need to be shamed by these that before us lie.'
He spoke, and sat and devoured the noisome food,
That his guest might heed his counsel, and find it good.

He who had passed his life in the upper sky,
Breathed in the breath of dawn, looked down on high
At the clouds beneath his wings, seen every beast
Obedient to his will; who had never ceased
With joy to return from journeying, on his way
Heaven upraising an arch of triumph; aye,
He who had ever the breast of partridge, quail,
Pheasant, to make him a warm and succulent meal;
That he should fall upon carrion and decay
And learn from a raven—faugh! disgust, dismay
Swarmed in his gorge. He reeled, and closed his eyes,
And called to mind how there, in the topmost skies,
Is victory to be found, and loveliness,
And love, and glory, and freedom limitless,
Eternal triumph, the joyous breath of the wind
At dawn. He opened his eyes, and could not find,

Wherever he stared, of those glories any trace;
All that he saw on every side was base,
Horrible, mean, revolting. With wings outspread
He sprang into air, and as departing, said:
'Forgive me, friend: live on for many a year
And joy in thy glorious ease, with thy carrion here
And miraculous length of days. Unworthy am I
To share this wonderful hospitality:
Keep thou thy noisome banquet! Be it my fate
To die in heaven's zenith, death I await
With resignation; I could never live on,
Doomed to grow old for ever on carrion!'

The king of heaven pinion-borne swept high
Aloft; the raven descried him with wondering eye
As he climbed upward and ever upward, till
His head was brushing the sun. On further still;
A moment he hung poised in that infinite blue
Canvas, a point seen; and was gone from view.

A. J. Arberry.

NEZAMI

Laili and Majnun
J. Atkinson

QAIS DECLARES HIS LOVE

Laili had, with her kindred, beenremoved
Among the Nijid mountains, where
She cherish'd still the thoughts of him she loved,
And her affection thus more deeply proved
Amid that wild retreat. Qais sought her there;
Sought her in rosy bower and silent glade,
Where the tall palm-trees flung refreshing shade,
He call'd upon her name again;
Again he call'd, alas! in vain;
His voice unheard, though raised on every side;
Echo alone to his lament replied;
And Laili! Laili! rang around,
As if enamour'd of that magic sound.
Dejected and forlorn, fast-falling dew
Glisten'd upon his cheeks of pallid hue;
Through grove and frowning glen he lonely stray'd,
And with his griefs the rocks were vocal made.
Beautiful Laili! had she gone for ever?–
Could he that thought support? oh, never, never!
Whilst deep emotion agonized his breast,
He to the morning breeze these words address'd:

'Breeze of the morn! so fresh and sweet,
Wilt thou my blooming mistress greet;
And, nestling in her glossy hair,
My tenderest thoughts, my love, declare?
Wilt thou, while mid her tresses sporting,
Their odorous balm, their perfume courting,

Say to that soul-seducing maid,
In grief how prostrate I am laid!
And gently whisper in her ear
This message, with an accent clear:
"Thy form is ever in my sight,
In thought by day, in dreams by night;
For one, in spirits sad and broken,
That mole would be the happiest token;
That mole which adds to every look
A magic spell I cannot brook;
For he who sees thy melting charms,
And does not feel his soul in arms,
Bursting with passion, rapture, all
That speak love's deepest, wildest thrall,
Must be, as Qaf's ice-summit, cold,
And, haply, scarce of human mould.
Let him, unmoved by charms like thine,
His worthless life at once resign—
Those lips are sugar, heavenly sweet;
Oh let but mine their pouting meet!
The balsam of delight they shed;
Their radiant colour ruby-red.
The Evil eye has struck my heart,
But thine in beauty sped the dart:
Thus many a flower, of richest hue,
Hath fall'n and perish'd where it grew;
Thy beauty is the sun in brightness,
Thy form a Peri's self in lightness;
A treasure thou, which, poets say,
The heavens would gladly steal away—
Too good, too pure, on earth to stay!'"

LAILI DISCONSOLATE

Laili in beauty, softness, grace,
Surpass'd the loveliest of her race;
She was a fresh and odorous flower,
Pluck'd by a fairy from her bower;

With heart-delighting rose-buds blooming,
The welcome breeze of spring perfuming.
The killing witchery that lies
In her soft, black, delicious eyes,
When gather'd in one amorous glance,
Pierces the heart, like sword or lance;
The prey that falls into her snare,
For life must mourn and struggle there;
Her eyelash speaks a thousand blisses,
Her lips of ruby ask for kisses;
Soft lips where sugar-sweetness dwells,
Sweet as the bee-hive's honey-cells;
Her cheeks, so beautiful and bright,
Had stole the moon's refulgent light;
Her form the cypress-tree expresses,
And full and ripe invites caresses;
With all these charms the heart to win,
There was a careless grief within–
Yet none beheld her grief, or heard;
She droop'd like broken-wingéd bird.
Her secret thoughts her love concealing,
But, softly to the terrace stealing,
From morn to eve she gazed around,
In hopes her Majnun might be found,
Wandering in sight. For she had none
To sympathize with her –not one!
None to compassionate her woes–
In dread of rivals, friends, and foes;
And though she smiled, her mind's distress
Fill'd all her thoughts with bitterness;
The fire of absence on them prey'd,
But light nor smoke that fire betray'd;
Shut up within herself, she sate,
Absorb'd in grief, disconsolate;
Yet true love has resources still,
Its soothing arts, and ever will!

QAIS IN THE DESERT

Who wanders near that palmy glade,
Where the fresh breeze adds coolness to the shade?
'Tis Majnun —he has left his father's tomb,
Again mid rocks and scorching plains to roam,
Unmindful of the sun's meridian heat,
Or the damp dewy night, with unshod feet;
Unmindful of the forest's savage brood,
Howling on every side in quest of blood;
No dread has he from aught of earth or air,
From den or aerie, calm in his despair:
He seems to court new perils, and can view
With unblench'd visage scenes of darkest hue;
Yet is he gentle, and his gracious mien
Checks the extended claw, where blood has been;
For tiger, wolf, and panther gather round
The maniac as their king, and lick the ground;
Fox and hyena fierce their snarling cease;
Lion and fawn familiar meet in peace;
Vulture and soaring eagle, on the wing,
Around his place of rest their shadows fling;
Like Solaiman, o'er all extends his reign;
His pillow is the lion's shaggy mane;
The wily leopard, on the herbage spread,
Forms like a carpet his romantic bed;
And lynx and wolf, in harmony combined,
Frisk o'er the sward, and gambol with the hind.
All pay their homage with respect profound,
As if in circles of enchantment bound.

THE DEATH OF LAILI

In summer all is bright and gay;
In autumn verdure fades away,
The trees assume a sickly hue,
Unnourish'd by the fragrant dew;
The genial sap, through numerous rills,
From root and branch and leaf distils;

But, drying in the chilly air,
The groves become despoil'd and bare;
Sapless, the garden's flowery pride
The winds disperse on every side,
And all that sight and smell delighted
Is by the ruthless season blighted.
So Laili's summer hours have pass'd;
And now she feels the autumnal blast;
Her bowers, her blooming bowers, assail'd,
The perfume of the rose exhaled,
Its wither'd leaves bestrew the ground
And desolation reigns around:
For, from the moment she beheld
Her lover's mental state unveil'd,
Her heart no consolation knew,
Deprived of hope's refreshing dew.
Ere that o'erwhelming misery came,
Thoughts of new life upheld her frame:
Amidst her bitterest weeping and distress,
Mid the dark broodings of her loneliness,
Though crush'd her feelings, and the man she loved
A wanderer of the forest, strangely moved,
Still was there hope, still was her mental gaze
Fix'd on the expected joys of after-days.
But now all hope had perish'd!—she had seen
The frenzied workings of that noble mien:
The fit delirious, the appalling start,
And grief and terror seized her trembling heart.
No tears she sheds, but pines away
   In deep entire despair;
The worm has seized its destined prey,
   The blight is on that face so fair,
And fearful symptoms of a swift decay
Come o'er her delicate frame, that in the strife
She almost sinks beneath the load of life.
Feeling the ebbing of the vital tide,
She calls her weeping mother to her side.
'Mother! my hour is come, thou need'st no longer chide;

For now no longer can my heart conceal
What once 'twas useless to reveal;
Yet, spite of thy affection, thou
May'st blame my fatal passion now.
But I have in my rapture quaff'd
Poison in love's delicious draught;
And feel the agony which sears
The soul, and dries the source of tears.
Oh mother! mother! all I crave,
When I am pillow'd in my grave,
Is that the anguish-stricken youth,
Whose wondrous constancy and truth
Blended our souls in one, may come
And weep upon his Laili's tomb.
Forbid him not; but let him there
Pour forth the flood of his despair,
And no unhallow'd step intrude
Upon his sacred solitude.
For he to me, my life, my stay,
Was precious as the light of day.
Amazing was his love sublime,
Which mock'd the wonted power of time;
And when thou see'st him grovelling near,
Wildly lamenting o'er my bier,
Frown not, but kindly, soothingly relate
Whate'er thou know'st of my disastrous fate.
Say to that woe-worn wanderer: "All is o'er;
Laili, thy own sad friend, is now no more;
From this world's heavy chains for ever free,
To thee her heart was given-she died for thee!
With love so blended was her life, so true
That glowing love, no other joy she knew.
No worldly cares her thoughts had e'er oppress'd:
The love of thee alone disturb'd her rest;
And in that love her gentle spirit pass'd,
Breathing on thee her blessing to the last.'"

The mournful mother gazed upon her child,
Now voiceless-though her lips imploring smiled;

Saw the dread change, the sudden pause of breath
Her beauty settled in the trance of death;
And, in the frenzy of her anguish, tore
Her hoary locks, the 'broider'd dress she wore;
Dissolved in tears, her wild and sorrowing cries
Brought down compassion from the weeping skies;
And so intense her grief, she shivering fell
Prostrate upon the corse, insensible,
And never, never rose again —the thread
Of life was broke —both, clasp'd together, dead!

THE DEATH OF QAIS

Again it was the task of faithful Zaid,
Through far-extending plain and forest wide,
To seek the man of many woes, and tell
The fate of her, alas! he loved so well,
Loved, doted on, until his mind, o'erwrought,
Was crush'd beneath intolerable thought.
With bleeding heart he found his lone abode,
Watering with tears the path on which he rode,
And beating his sad breast; Majnun perceived
His friend approach, and ask'd him why he grieved;
What withering sorrow on his cheek had prey'd,
And why in melancholy black array'd.
'Alas!' he cried, 'the hail has crush'd my bowers;
A sudden storm has blighted all my flowers;
Thy cypress-tree o'erthrown, the leaves are sear;
The moon has fallen from her lucid sphere;
Laili is dead!' No sooner was the word
Utter'd, no sooner the dread tidings heard,
Than Majnun, sudden as the lightning's stroke
Sank on the ground, unconscious, with the shock,
And there lay motionless, as if his life
Had been extinguish'd in that mortal strife.
But, soon recovering, he prepared to rise,
Rewaken'd frenzy glaring in his eyes,

And, starting on his feet, a hollow groan
Burst from his heart. 'Now, now I *am* alone!
Why hast thou harrowing words like these express'd?
Why hast thou plunged a dagger in my breast?
Away! away!' The savage beasts around
In a wide circle couch'd upon the ground,
Wondering look'd on, whilst furiously he rent
His tatter'd garments, and his loud lament
Rang through the echoing forest. Now he threads
The mazes of the shadowy wood, which spreads
Perpetual gloom, and now emerges where
Nor bower nor grove obstructs the fiery air;
Climbs to the mountain's brow, o'er hill and plain
Urged quicker onwards by his burning brain,
Across the desert's arid boundary hies;
Zaid, like his shadow, following where he flies;
And when the tomb of Laili meets his view,
Prostrate he falls, the ground his tears bedew;
Rolling distraught, he spreads his arms to clasp
The sacred temple, writhing like an asp:
Despair and horror swell his ceaseless moan,
And still he clasps the monumental stone.
'Alas!' he cries—'No more shall I behold
That angel-face, that form of heavenly mould.
She was the rose I cherish'd —but a gust
Of blighting wind has laid her in the dust.
She was my favourite cypress, full of grace,
But death has snatch'd her from her biding-place.
The tyrant has deprived me of the flower
I planted in my own sequester'd bower;
The Basil sweet, the choicest ever seen,
Cruelly torn and scatter'd o'er the green.
O beauteous flower! nipp'd by the winter's cold,
Gone from a world thou never didst behold.
O bower of joy! with blossoms fresh and fair,
But doom'd, alas! no ripen'd fruit to bear.
Where shall I find thee now, in darkness shrouded!
Those eyes of liquid light for ever clouded!

Where those carnation lips, that musky mole
Upon thy cheek, that treasure of the soul!
Though hidden from my view those charms of thine,
Still do they bloom in this fond heart of mine;
Though far removed from all I held so dear,
Though all I loved on earth be buried here,
Remembrance to the past enchantment gives,
Memory, blest memory, in my heart still lives.
Yes! thou hast quitted this contentious life,
This scene of endless treachery and strife;
And I like thee shall soon my fetters burst,
And quench in draughts of heavenly love my thirst:
There, where angelic bliss can never cloy,
We soon shall meet in everlasting joy;
The taper of our souls, more clear and bright,
Will then be lustrous with immortal light!'
He ceased, and from the tomb to which he clung
Suddenly to a distance wildly sprung,
And, seated on his camel, took the way
Leading to where his father's mansion lay;
His troop of vassal-beasts, as usual, near,
With still unchanged devotion, front and rear;
Yet, all unconscious, reckless where he went,
The sport of passion, on no purpose bent,
He sped along, or stopp'd; the woods and plains
Resounding with his melancholy strains;
Such strains as from a broken spirit flow,
The wailings of unmitigated woe;
But the same frenzy which had fired his mind
Strangely to leave his Laili's grave behind
Now drove him back, and with augmented grief,
All sighs and tears, and hopeless of relief,
He flings himself upon the tomb again,
As if he there for ever would remain,
Fatally mingled with the dust beneath,
The young, the pure, the beautiful in death.
Closely he strain'd the marble to his breast,
A thousand kisses eagerly impress'd,

And knock'd his forehead in such desperate mood,
The place around him was distain'd with blood.
Alone, unseen; his vassals keep remote
Curious intruders from that sacred spot;
Alone, with wasted form and sombre eyes.
Groaning in anguish he exhausted lies;
No more life's joys or miseries will he meet,
Nothing to rouse him from this last retreat;
Upon a sinking gravestone he is laid,
The gates already opening for the dead!
Selim, the generous, who had twice before
Sought his romantic refuge, to implore
The wanderer to renounce the life he led,
And shun the ruin bursting o'er his head,
Again explored the wilderness, again
Cross'd craggy rock, deep glen, and dusty plain
To find his new abode. A month had pass'd
Mid mountain wild, when, turning back, at last
He spied the wretched sufferer alone,
Stretch'd on the ground, his head upon a stone.
Majnun, up-gazing, recognized his face,
And bade his growling followers give him place;
Then said: 'Why art thou here again, since thou
Left me in wrath? What are thy wishes now?
I am a wretch bow'd down with bitterest woe,
Doom'd the extremes of misery to know,
Whilst thou, in affluence born, in pleasure nursed,
Stranger to ills the direst and the worst,
Can never join, unless in mockery,
With one so lost to all the world as me!'
Salim replied: 'Fain would I change thy will,
And bear thee hence —be thy companion still:
Wealth shall be thine, and peace and social joy,
And tranquil days, no sorrow to annoy;
And she for whom thy soul has yearn'd so long
May yet be gain'd, and none shall do thee wrong.'
Deeply he groan'd, and wept: 'No more, no more!
Speak not of her whose memory I adore;

She whom I loved, than life itself more dear,
My friend, my angel-bride, is buried here!
Dead!—but her spirit is now in heaven, whilst I
Live, and am dead with grief-yet do not die.
This is the fatal spot, my Laili's tomb—
This the lamented place of martyrdom.
Here lies my life's sole treasure, life's sole trust;
All that was bright in beauty gone to dust!'
Selim before him in amazement stood,
Stricken with anguish, weeping tears of blood;
And consolation blandly tried to give.
What consolation? Make his Laili live?
His gentle words and looks were only found
To aggravate the agonizing wound;
And weeks in fruitless sympathy had pass'd,
But, patient still, he linger'd to the last;
Then, with an anxious heart, of hope bereft,
The melancholy spot, reluctant, left.
The life of Majnun had received its blight;
His troubled day was closing fast in night.
Still weeping, bitter, bitter tears he shed,
As grovelling in the dust his hands he spread
In holy prayer. 'O God! Thy servant hear!
And in Thy gracious mercy set him free
From the afflictions which oppress him here,
That, in the Prophet's name, he may return to Thee!'
Thus murmuring, on the tomb he laid his head,
And with a sigh his wearied spirit fled.

ENVOI

O ye, who thoughtlessly repose
On what this flattering world bestows,
Reflect how transient is your stay!
How soon e'en sorrow fades away!
The pangs of grief the heart may wring
In life, but Heaven removes the sting;
The world to come makes bliss secure—
The world to come, eternal, pure.

What other solace for the human soul,
But everlasting rest—virtue's unvarying goal!
SAKI! Nezami's strain is sung;
The Persian poet's pearls are strung;
Then fill again the goblet high!
Thou wouldst not ask the reveller why?
Fill to the love that changes never!
Fill to the love that lives for ever!
That, purified by earthly woes,
At last with bliss seraphic glows.

ATTAR

The Bird-Parliament
Edward FitzGerald

PRELUDE

Once on a time from all the Circles seven
Between the steadfast Earth and rolling Heaven
THE BIRDS, of all Note, Plumage, and Degree,
That float in Air, and roost upon the Tree;
And they that from the Waters snatch their Meat,
And they that scour the Desert with long Feet:
Birds of all Natures, known or not to Man,
Flock'd from all Quarters into full Divan,
On no less solemn business than to find,
Or choose, a Sultan Khalif of their kind,
For whom, if never theirs, or lost, they pined.
The Snake had his, 'twas said; and so the Beast
His Lion-lord; and Man had his, at least;
And that the Birds, who nearest were the Skies,
And went apparell'd in its Angel Dyes,
Should be without—under no better Law
Than that which lost all other in the Maw—
Disperst without a Bond of Union—nay,
Or meeting to make each the other's Prey—

The San'an Sheikh, unsigned, 18×30 cm., about 1960

Autumn of Khayyam, Hosain Behzad, 43×63 cm., 1947

This was the Grievance—this the solemn Thing
On which the scatter'd Commonwealth of Wing,
From all the four Winds, flying like to Cloud
That met and blacken'd Heav'n, and Thunder-loud
With Sound of whirring Wings and Beaks that clash'd,
Down like a Torrent on the Desert dash'd:
Till by Degrees, the Hubbub and Pell-mell
Into some Order and Precedence fell,
And, Proclamation made of Silence, each
In special Accent, but in general Speech
That all should understand, as seem'd him best,
The Congregation of all Wings addrest.

And first, with Heart so full as from his Eyes
Ran weeping, up rose Tajidar the Wise;
The mystic Mark upon whose Bosom show'd
That He alone of all the Birds THE ROAD
Had travell'd; and the Crown upon his Head
Had reach'd the Goal; and He stood forth and said:
'O Birds, by what Authority divine
I speak you know by *His* authentic Sign
And Name, emblazon'd on my Breast and Bill;
Whose Counsel I assist at, and fulfil:
At His Behest I measured as he plann'd
The Spaces of the Air and Sea and Land;
I gauged the secret sources of the Springs
From Cloud to Fish; the Shadow of my Wings
Dream'd over sleeping Deluge; piloted
The Blast that bore Solaiman's Throne; and led
The Clouds of Birds that canopied his Head;
Whose Word I brought to Belqais: and I shared
The Counsel that with Asaf he prepared.
And now *you* want a Khalif; and I know
Him, and his whereabout, and How to go;
And go alone I could, and plead your cause
Alone for all; but, by the eternal laws,
Yourselves by Toil and Travel of your own
Must for your old Delinquency atone.

Were you indeed not blinded by the Curse
Of Self-exile, that still grows worse and worse,
Yourselves would know that, though *you* see him not,
He *is* with you this Moment, on this Spot,
Your Lord through all Forgetfulness and Crime,
Here, There, and Everywhere, and through all Time.
But as a Father, whom some wayward Child
By sinful Self-will has unreconciled,
Waits till the sullen Reprobate at cost
Of long Repentance should regain the Lost;
Therefore, yourselves to see as you are seen,
Yourselves must bridge the Gulf you made between
By such a Search and Travel, to be gone
Up to the mighty mountain Qaf, whereon
Hinges the World, and round about whose Knees
Into one Ocean mingle the Sev'n Seas;
In whose impenetrable Forest-folds
Of Light and Dark 'Simorgh' his Presence holds;
Not to be reach'd, if to be reach'd at all,
But by a Road the stoutest might appal;
Of Travel not of Days or Months, but Years–
Lifelong perhaps; of Dangers, Doubts, and Fears
As yet unheard -of; Sweat of Blood and Brain
Interminable –often all in vain–
And, if successful, no Return again:
A Road whose very Preparation scared
The Traveller who yet must be prepared.
Who then this Travel to Result would bring
Needs both a Lion's Heart beneath the Wing,
And even more, a Spirit purified
Of Worldly Passion, Malice, Lust, and Pride:
Yea, ev'n of Worldly Wisdom, which grows dim
And dark, the nearer it approaches *Him*,
Who to the Spirit's Eye alone reveal'd,
By sacrifice of Wisdom's self unseal'd;
Without which none who reach the Place could bear
To look upon the Glory dwelling there.'

THE NIGHTINGALE

Then came *The Nightingale,* from such a Draught
Of Ecstasy that from the Rose he quaff'd
Reeling as drunk, and ever did distil
In exquisite Divisions from his Bill
To inflame the Hearts of Men—and thus sang He:
'To me alone, alone, is giv'n the Key
Of Love; of whose whole Mystery possesst,
When I reveal a little to the Rest,
Forthwith Creation listening forsakes
The Reins of Reason, and my Frenzy takes:
Yea, whosoever once has quaff'd this wine
He leaves unlisten'd David's Song for mine.
In vain do Men for my Divisions strive,
And die themselves making dead Lutes alive:
I hang the Stars with Meshes for Men's Souls:
The Garden underneath my Music rolls.
The long, long Morns that mourn the Rose away
I sit in silence, and on Anguish prey:
But the first Air which the New Year shall breathe
Up to my Boughs of Message from beneath
That in her green Harim my Bride unveils,
My Throat bursts silence and *her* Advent hails,
Who in her crimson Volume registers
The Notes of Him whose Life is lost in hers.
The Rose I love and worship now is here;
If dying, yet reviving, Year by Year;
But that you tell of, all my Life why waste
In vainly searching; or, if found, not taste?'

So with Division infinite and Trill
On would the Nightingale have warbled still
And all the World have listen'd ; but a Note
Of sterner Import check'd the lovesick Throat.

'Oh watering with thy melodious Tears
Love's Garden, and who dost indeed the Ears
Of men with thy melodious Fingers mould
As David's Finger Iron did of old:
Why not, like David, dedicate thy Dower
Of Song to something better than a Flower?
Empress indeed of Beauty, so they say,
But one whose Empire hardly lasts a Day,
By Insurrection of the Morning's Breath
That made her hurried to Decay and Death;
And while she lasts contented to be seen,
And worshipt, for the Garden's only Queen,
Leaving thee singing on thy Bough forlorn,
Or if she smile on Thee, perhaps in Scorn.'

THE PARROT

Then came the subtle *Parrot* in a coat
Greener than Greensward, and about his Throat
A Collar ran of sub-sulphureous Gold;
And in his Beak a Sugarplum he troll'd,
That all his Words with luscious Lisping ran,
And to this Tune: 'Oh cruel Cage, and Man
More iron still who did confine me there,
Who else with him whose Livery I wear
Ere this to his Eternal Fount had been,
And drunk what should have kept me evergreen.
But now I know the Place, and I am free
To go, and all the Wise will follow Me.
Some' —and upon the Nightingale one Eye
He leer'd—'for nothing but the Blossom sigh:
But I am for the luscious Pulp that grows
Where, and for which the Blossom only blows:
And which so long as the Green Tree provides
What better grows along Qaf's dreary Sides?
And what more needful Prophet *there* than He
Who gives me Life to nip it from the Tree?'

To whom the Tajidar: 'O thou whose Best
In the green leaf of Paradise is drest,
But whose Neck kindles with a lower Fire—
Oh slip the collar off of base Desire,
And stand apparell'd in Heav'n's Woof entire!
This Life that hangs so sweet about your Lips,
But, spite of all your Khezr, slips and slips,
What is it but itself the coarser Rind
Of the True Life withinside and behind,
Which he shall never never reach unto
Till the gross Shell of Carcase he break through?'

THE RING-DOVE

Then from a Wood was heard unseen to coo
The *Ring-dove*: 'Yusof! Yusof! Yusof! Yu—'
(For thus her sorrow broke her Note in twain,
And, just where broken, took it up again)
'sof! Yusof! Yusof! Yusof!'—But one Note,
Which still repeating, she made hoarse her throat,
Till checkt: 'Oh You, who with your idle Sighs
Block up the Road of better Enterprise:
Sham Sorrow all, or bad as sham if true,
When once the better thing is come to *do*;
Beware lest wailing thus you meet *his* Doom
Who all too long his Darling wept, from whom
You draw the very Name you hold so dear,
And which the World is somewhat tired to hear.'

THE EXCUSES

And after these came others—arguing,
Inquiring, and excusing—some one Thing,
And some another—endless to repeat,
But, in the Main, Sloth, Folly, or Deceit.
Their Souls were to the vulgar Figure cast
Of earthly Victual not of Heavenly Fast.

At last one smaller Bird, of a rare kind,
Of modest Plume and unpresumptuous Mind,
Whisper'd: 'Oh Tajidar, we know indeed
How Thou both knowest, and would'st help our Need;
For thou art wise and holy, and hast been
Behind the Veil, and there *The Presence* seen.
But we are weak and vain, with little care
Beyond our yearly Nests and daily Fare
How should we reach the Mountain? and if there
How get so great a Prince to hear our Prayer?
For there, you say, dwells *The Simorgh* alone
In Glory, like Solaiman on his Throne,
And we but Pismires at his feet: can He
Such puny Creatures stoop to hear, or see;
Or hearing, seeing, *own* us—unakin
As He to Folly, Woe, and Death, and Sin?'—

To whom the Tajidar, whose Voice for those
Bewilder'd ones to full Compassion rose:
'Oh lost so long in Exile, you disclaim
The very Fount of Being whence you came,
Cannot be parted from, and, will or no,
Whether for Good or Evil must reflow!
For look-the Shadows into which the Light
Of his pure Essence down by infinite
Gradation dwindles, which at random play
Through Space in Shape indefinite—one Ray
Of his Creative *Will* into *defined*
Creation quickens: We that swam the Wind,
And they the Flood below, and Man and Beast
That walk between, from Lion to the least
Pismire that creeps along Solaiman's Wall—
Yea, that in which they swim, fly, walk, and crawl—
However near the Fountain Light, or far
Removed, yet *His* authentic Shadows are;
Dead Matter's Self but the dark Residue
Exterminating Glory dwindles to.

A Mystery too fearful in the Crowd
To utter —scarcely to Thyself aloud—
But when in solitary Watch and Prayer
Consider'd: and religiously beware
Lest Thou the Copy with the Type confound;
And *Deity,* with Deity indrown'd—
For as pure Water into purer Wine
Incorporating shall itself refine
While the dull Drug lies half resolved below,
With Him and with his Shadows it is so:
The baser Forms, to whatsoever Change
Subject, still vary through their lower Range:
To which the *higher* even shall decay,
That, letting ooze their better Part away
For Things of Sense and Matter, in the End
Shall merge into the Clay to which they tend.
Unlike to him, who straining through the Bond
Of outward Being for a Life beyond,
While the gross Worldling to *his* Centre clings,
That draws him deeper in, exulting springs
To merge him in the central *Soul* of Things.
And shall not he pass home with other Zest
Who, with full Knowledge, yearns for such a Rest,
Than he, who with his better self at strife,
Drags on the weary Exile call'd *This Life?*—
One, like a child with outstretcht Arms and Face
Upturn'd, anticipates his Sire's Embrace;
The other crouching like a guilty Slave
Till flogg'd to Punishment across the Grave.
And, knowing that *His* glory ill can bear
The unpurged Eye; do thou Thy Breast prepare;
And the mysterious Mirror He set there,
To temper his reflected Image in,
Clear of Distortion, Doubleness, and Sin:
And in thy Conscience understanding *this*,
The *Double* only *seems*, but The *One is*,
Thyself to Self-annihilation give
That this false *Two* in that true *One* may live.

For this I say: if, looking in thy Heart,
Thou for *Self-whole* mistake thy *Shadow-part*,
That Shadow-part indeed into *The Sun*
Shall melt, but senseless of its Union:
But in that Mirror if with purgéd eyes
Thy Shadow Thou *for* Shadow recognize,
Then shalt Thou back into thy Centre fall,
A conscious Ray of that eternal *All*.'

ATTAINMENT

Till of the mighty Host that fledged the Dome
Of Heav'n and Floor of Earth on leaving Home,
A Handful reach'd and scrambled up the Knees
Of Qaf whose Feet dip in the Seven Seas;
And of the few that up his Forest-sides
Of Light and Darkness where *The Presence* hides,
But *Thirty* –thirty desperate draggled Things,
Half dead, with scarce a Feather on their Wings,
Stunn'd, blinded, deafen'd with the Crash and Craze
Of Rock and Sea collapsing in a Blaze
That struck the Sun to Cinder –fell upon
The Threshold of the Everlasting *One*,
With but enough of Life in each to cry,
On THAT which all absorb'd.
And suddenly
Forth flash'd a wingéd Harbinger of Flame
And Tongue of Fire, and 'Who?' and 'Whence they came?'
And 'Why?' demanded. And the Tajidar
For all the Thirty answer'd him: 'We are
Those Fractions of the Sum of Being, far
Dis-spent and foul disfigured, that once more
Strike for Admission at the Treasury Door.'

To whom the Angel answer'd: 'Know ye not
That He you seek recks little who or what
Of Quantity and Kind –himself the Fount
Of Being Universal needs no Count

Of all the Drops o'erflowing from his Urn,
In what Degree they issue or return?'
Then cried the Spokesman: 'Be it even so:
Let us but see the Fount from which we flow,
And, seeing, lose Ourselves therein!' And Lo!
Before the Word was utter'd, or the Tongue
Of Fire replied, or Portal open flung,
They were *within* —they were before the Throne,
Before the Majesty that sat thereon,
But wrapt in so insufferable a Blaze
Of Glory as beat down their baffled Gaze,
Which, downward dropping, fell upon a Scroll
That, Lightning-like, flash'd back on each the whole
Past half-forgotten Story of his Soul:
Like that which Yusof in his Glory gave
His Brethren as some Writing he would have
Interpreted; and at a Glance, behold
Their own Indenture for their Brother sold!
And so with these poor Thirty; who, abasht
In Memory all laid bare and Conscience lasht,
By full Confession and Self-loathing flung
The Rags of carnal Self that round them clung;
And, their old selves self-knowledged and self-loathed,
And in the Soul's Integrity reclothed,
Once more they ventured from the Dust to raise
Their Eyes—up to the Throne—into the Blaze,
And in the Centre of the Glory there
Beheld the Figure of—*Themselves*—as 'twere
Transfigured—looking to Themselves, beheld
The Figure on the Throne en-miracled,
Until their Eyes themselves and *That* between
Did hesitate which *Seer* was, which *Seen*;
They That, That They: Another, yet the Same;
Dividual, yet One: from whom there came
A Voice of awful Answer, scarce discern'd,
From *which* to Aspiration *whose* return'd
They scarcely knew; as when some Man apart
Answers aloud the Question in his Heart:

'The Sun of my Perfection is a Glass
Wherein from *Seeing* into *Being* pass
All who, reflecting as reflected see
Themselves in Me, and Me in them: not *Me*,
But all of Me that a contracted Eye
Is comprehensive of Infinity;
Nor yet *Themselves*: no Selves, but of The All
Fractions, from which they split and whither fall.
As Water lifted from the Deep, again
Falls back in individual Drops of Rain,
Then melts into the Universal Main.
All you have been, and seen, and done, and thought,
Not You but I, have seen and been and wrought:
I was the Sin that from Myself rebell'd;
I the Remorse that tow'rd Myself compell'd;
I was the Tajidar who led the Track;
I was the little Briar that pull'd you back:
Sin and Contrition –Retribution owed,
And cancell'd –Pilgrim, Pilgrimage, and Road,
Was but Myself toward Myself; and Your
Arrival but *Myself* at my own Door;
Who in your Fraction of Myself behold
Myself within the Mirror Myself hold
To see Myself in, and each part of Me
That sees himself, though drown'd, shall ever see.
Come you lost Atoms to your Centre draw,
And *be* the Eternal Mirror that you saw:
Rays that have wander'd into Darkness wide
Return, and back into your Sun subside.'

This was the Parliament of Birds; and this
The Story of the Host who went amiss,
And of the Few that better Upshot found;
Which being now recounted, Lo, the Ground
Of Speech fails underfoot: But this to tell–
Their Road is thine –Follow– and Fare thee well.

JAMI

Salaman and Absal
Edward FitzGerald

PRELIMINARY INVOCATION

O Thou, whose Spirit through this universe
In which Thou dost involve thyself diffused,
Shall so perchance irradiate human clay
That men suddenly dazzled, lose themselves
In ecstasy before a mortal shrine
Whose Light is but a Shade of the Divine;
Not till thy Secret Beauty through the cheek
Of LAILI smite doth she inflame MAJNUN
And not till Thou have kindled SHIRIN's Eyes
The hearts of those two Rivals swell with blood.
For Lov'd and Lover are not but by Thee,
Nor Beauty—mortal Beauty but the veil
Thy Heavenly hides behind, and from itself
Feeds, and our hearts yearn after as a Bride
That glances past us veil'd —but ever so
That none the veil from what it hides may know.
How long wilt thou continue thus the World
To cozen with the phantom of a veil
From which thou only peepest? I would be
Thy Lover, and thine only—I, mine eyes
Seal'd in the light of Thee to all but Thee,
Yea, in the revelation of Thyself
Lost to Myself, and all that Self is not
Within the Double world that is but One.
Thou lurkest under all the forms of Thought,
Under the form of all Created things;
Look where I may, still nothing I discern
But Thee throughout this Universe, wherein
Thyself Thou dost reflect, and through those eyes
Of him whom MAN thou madest, scrutinize.

To thy Harim DIVIDUALITY
No entrance finds —no word of THIS and THAT;
Do Thou my separate and derivéd Self
Make one with thy Essential! Leave me room
On that Divan which leaves no room for Twain;
Lest, like the simple Arab in the tale,
I grow perplext, oh God! 'twixt 'ME' and 'THEE';
If *I* —this Spirit that inspires me whence?
If THOU —then what this sensual Impotence?

THE SIMPLE ARAB

From the solitary Desert
Up to Bagdad came a simple
  Arab; there amid the rout
Grew bewildered of the countless
People, hither, thither, running,
Coming, going, meeting, parting,
Clamour, clatter, and confusion,
    All about him and about.
Travel-wearied, hubbub-dizzy,
Would the simple Arab fain
Get to sleep —'But then, on waking,
How,' quoth he, 'amid so many
  Waking know Myself again?'
So, to make the matter certain,
Strung a gourd about his ankle,
And, into a corner creeping,
Bagdad and Himself and People
  Soon were blotted from his brain.
But one that heard him and divin'd
His purpose, slily crept behind;
From the Sleeper's ankle slipping,
  Round his own the pumpkin tied,
  And laid him down to sleep beside.
By and by the Arab waking
Looks directly for his Signal—
Sees it on another's Ankle—

Cries aloud: 'Oh Good-for-nothing
Rascal to perplex me so!
That by you I am bewilder'd,
Whether I be I or no!
If I –the Pumpkin why on You?
If You –then Where am I, and WHO?'

THE BIRTH OF SALAMAN

The SAGE his satire ended; and THE SHAH,
Determin'd on his purpose, but the means
Resigning to Supreme Intelligence,
With Magic-mighty Wisdom his own WILL
Colleagued, and wrought his own accomplishment.
For Lo! from Darkness came to Light A CHILD,
Of carnal composition unattaint;
A Perfume from the realm of Wisdom wafted;
A Rose-bud blowing on the Royal stem;
The crowning Jewel of the Crown; a Star
Under whose augury triumph'd the Throne.
For whom dividing, and again in one
Whole perfect Jewel reuniting, those
Twin Jewel-words, SALAMAT and ASMAN,
They hail'd him by the title of SALAMAN.
And whereas from no Mother milk he drew,
They chose for him a Nurse –her name ABSAL–
So young, the opening roses of her breast
But just had budded to an infant's lip;
So beautiful, as from the silver line
Dividing the musk-harvest of her hair
Down to her foot that trampled crowns of Kings,
A Moon of beauty full; who thus elect
Should in the garmet of her bounty fold
SALAMAN of auspicious augury,
Should feed him with the flowing of her breast.
And, once her eyes had open'd upon Him,
They closed to all the world beside, and fed
For ever doting on her Royal jewel

Close in his golden cradle casketed:
Opening and closing which her day's delight,
To gaze upon his heart-inflaming cheek—
Upon the Babe whom, if she could, she would
Have cradled as the Baby of her eye.
In rose and musk she wash'd him—to his lip
Press'd the pure sugar from the honeycomb;
And when, day over, she withdrew her milk,
She made, and having laid him in, his bed,
Burn'd all night like a taper o'er his head.

ABSAL TEMPTS SALAMAN

And now the cypress stature of Salaman
Had reached his top, and now to blossom full
The garden of his Beauty: and Absal,
Fairest of hers, as of his fellows he
The fairest, long'd to gather from the tree.
But, for that flower upon the lofty stem
Of Glory grew to which her hand fell short,
To conjure as she might within her reach.
The darkness of her eyes she darken'd round
With surma, to benight him in mid day,
And over them adorn'd and arch'd the bows
To wound him there when lost; her musky locks
Into so many snaky ringlets curl'd
In which Temptation nestled o'er the cheek,
Which rose she kindled with vermilion dew,
And then one subtle grain of musk laid there,
The bird of that belovéd heart to snare.
Sometimes in passing with a laugh would break
The pearl-enclosing ruby of her lips;
Or, busied in the room, as by mischance
Would let the lifted sleeve disclose awhile
The vein of silver running up within;
Or, rising as in haste, her golden anklets
Clash, at whose sudden summons to bring down
Under her silver feet the golden Crown.

Thus, by innumerable witcheries,
She went about soliciting his eyes,
Through which she knew the robber unaware
Steals in, and takes the bosom by surprise.

THE LOVERS FLEE

Six days SALAMAN on the Camel rode,
And then the hissing arrows of reproof
Were fallen far behind; and on the Seventh
He halted on the Seashore; on the shore
Of a great Sea that reaching like a floor
Of rolling Firmament below the Sky's
From QAF to QAF, to GAU and MAHI down
Descended, and its Stars were living eyes.
The Face of it was as it were a range
Of moving Mountains; or a countless host
Of Camels trooping tumultuously up,
Host over host, and foaming at the lip.
Within, innumerable glittering things
Sharp as cut Jewels, to the sharpest eye
Scarce visible, hither and hither slipping,
As silver scissors slice a blue brocade;
But should the Dragon coil'd in the abyss
Emerge to light, his starry counter-sign
Would shrink into the depth of Heav'n aghast.

SALAMAN eyed the moving wilderness
On which he thought, once launcht, no foot nor eye
Should ever follow; forthwith he devis'd
Of sundry scented woods along the shore
A little shallop like a Quarter-moon,
Wherein Absal and He like Sun and Moon
Enter'd as into some Celestial Sign;
That, figured like a bow, but arrow-like
In flight, was feather'd with a little sail,
And, pitcht upon the water like a duck,
So with her bosom sped to her Desire.

When they had sailed their vessel for a Moon,
And marr'd their beauty with the wind o' the Sea,
Suddenly in mid sea reveal'd itself
An Isle, beyond imagination fair;
An Isle that all was Garden; not a Flower,
Nor Bird of plumage like the flower, but there;
Some like the Flower, and others like the Leaf;
Some, as the Pheasant and the Dove adorn'd
With crown and collar, over whom, alone,
The jewell'd Peacock like a Sultan shone;
While the Musicians, and among them Chief
The Nightingale, sang hidden in the trees
Which, arm in arm, from fingers quivering
With any breath of air, fruit of all kind
Down scatter'd in profusion to their feet,
Where fountains of sweet water ran between,
And Sun and shadow chequer-chased the green.
Here Eram-garden seem'd in secrecy
Blowing the rose-bud of his Revelation;
Or Paradise, forgetful of the dawn
Of Audit, lifted from her face the veil.

SALAMAN saw the Isle, and thought no more
Of Further —there with ABSAL he sate down,
ABSAL and He together side by side,
Together like the Lily and the Rose,
Together like the Soul and Body, one.
Under its trees in one another's arms
They slept —they drank its fountains hand in hand—
Paraded with the Peacock —raced the Partridge—
Chased the green Parrot for his stolen fruit,
Or sang divisions with the Nightingale.
There was the Rose without a thorn, and there
The Treasure and no Serpent to beware—
Oh think of such a Mistress at your side
In such a Solitude, and none to chide!

Sa'di and the cupbearer, Hosain Behzad, 25×21 cm., 1958

The General Office of Bonyad Museums

Meeting, Hosain Behzad, 49×59 cm., 1953

THE BURNING OF ABSAL

SALAMAN bow'd his forehead to the dust
Before his Father; to his Father's hand
Fast —but yet fast, and faster, to his own
Clung one, who by no tempest of reproof
Or wrath might be dissever'd from the stem
She grew to: till, between Remorse and Love,
He came to loathe his Life and long for Death.
And, as from him *She* would not be divorc'd,
With Her he fled again: he fled —but now
To no such Island centred in the sea
As lull'd them into Paradise before;
But to the Solitude of Desolation,
The Wilderness of Death. And as before
Of sundry scented woods along the shore
A shallop he devised to carry them
Over the water whither foot nor eye
Should ever follow them, he thought-so now
Of sear wood strewn about the plain of Death,
A raft to bear them through the wave of Fire
Into Annihilation, he devis'd,
Gather'd, and built; and, firing with a Torch,
Into the central flame ABSAL and He
Sprung hand in hand exulting. But the SAGE
In secret all had order'd; and the Flame,
Directed by his self-fulfilling WILL,
Devouring Her to ashes, left untouch'd
SALAMAN—all the baser metal burn'd,
And to itself the authentic Gold return'd.

.....

SALAMAN fired the pile; and in the flame
That, passing him, consumed ABSAL like straw,
Died his Divided Self, his Individual
Surviv'd, and, like a living Soul from which
The Body falls, strange, naked, and alone.

Then rose his cry to Heaven —his eyelashes
Wept blood—his sighs stood like a smoke in Heaven,
And Morning rent her garment at his anguish.
And when Night came, that drew the pen across
The written woes of Day for all but him,
Crouch'd in a lonely corner of the house,
He seem'd to feel about him in the dark
For one who was not, and whom no fond word
Could summon from the Void in which she lay.

And so the Wise One found him where he sate
Bow'd down alone in darkness; and once more
Made the long-silent voice of Reason sound
In the deserted Palace of his Soul;
Until SALAMAN lifted up his head
To bow beneath the Master; sweet it seem'd,
Sweeping the chaff and litter from his own,
To be the very dust of Wisdom's door,
Slave of the Farman of the Lord of Life,
Who pour'd the wine of Wisdom in his cup,
Who laid the dew of Peace upon his lips:
Yea, wrought by Miracle in his behalf.
For when old Love return'd to Memory,
And broke in passion from his lips, THE SAGE,
Under whose waxing WILL Existence rose
From Nothing, and, relaxing, waned again,
Raising a phantom Image of ABSAL,
Set it awhile before SALAMAN's eyes,
Till, having sow'd the seed of comfort there,
It went again down to Annihilation.
But ever, as the phantom past away,
THE SAGE would tell of a Celestial Love;
'ZOHREH,' he said, 'ZOHREH, compared with whom
That brightest star that bears her name in Heav'n
Was but a winking taper; and ABSAL,
Queen-star of Beauties in this world below,
But her distorted image in the stream
Of fleeting Matter; and all Eloquence,

And Soul-enchaining harmonies of Song,
A far-off echo of that Harp in Heav'n
Which Dervish-dances to her harmony.'

SALAMAN listen'd, and inclin'd —again
Entreated, inclination ever grew;
Until THE SAGE beholding in his Soul
The SPIRIT quicken, so effectually
With ZOHREH wrought, that she reveal'd herself
In her pure lustre to SALAMAN'S Soul,
And blotting ABSAL'S Image from his breast,
There reign'd instead. Celestial Beauty seen,
He left the Earthly; and, once come to know
Eternal Love, the Mortal he let go.

EPIC

FERDOWSI

SATIRE ON MAHMOUD

Think not, O King! thy sceptre or thy pow'r
One moment can arrest the destin'd hour;
Know, 'tis thy charge pre-eminently thine
To act with justice, moral and divine.
The ant has life, that culls the bearded grain,
Thou shall not dare to sorrow it with pain.
Didst thou not tremble, conscious that the muse
Wou'd eminently scorn thy sordid views?
Didst thou not fear the man, whose heav'nly strain,
Bounding o'er time, made monarchs rule again–
Had worth or judgment glimmer'd in your soul,
You had not basely all my honour stole–
Had royal blood flow'd in your grov'ling veins,
A monarch's laurels had adorn'd my strains.
Or were your mother not ignobly base,
The slave of lust–thou first of all thy race–
A poet's merit had inspir'd thy mind,
By science tutor'd, and by worth refin'd–
Such as thou art, the vileness of thy birth
Precludes each generous sentiment of worth–
Nor Kingly origin, nor noble race,
Warms thy low heart, the offspring of disgrace–
Thy life poor wretch! 'twas Isfahan that gave,
Thy sire a blacksmith, and thy dam a slave.
This lesson, let each moralist indite,
Ne'er strive to make an *Ethiopian* white–
Nor vainly think the bastard of a slave
Can emulate the feelings of the brave–
Can the base prostitute with virtue glow,
Or worth can her polluted lineage know?–

For thee, will nature from her order stray,
And give to night the sun's meridian ray?—
In smoothest streams my numbers richly flow,
Now glide along, and now with rapture glow.
Lives there a poet in whose tuneful veins
Flow loftier thoughts in more poetic strains?
Tho' poor, tho' humble—still the voice of fame
Shall eternize Ferdowsi's laurell'd name—
Heroes have blaz'd, the meteor of an hour,
Oblivion menac'd to entomb their pow'r—
Till snatch'd from silence, from devouring time,
They reign for ever, in the verse sublime—
For thirty years I woo'd the tuneful Nine,
And Persia lives in my immortal line—
But when alas! I clos'd the grand design
(The royal word was pledg'd, that word divine—
To monarchs sacred) vainly did I deem
That honour and rewards wou'd grace my theme—
So base a gift thou meanly dar'd to send
(Stamp'd for thy falsehood, wither'd be thy end)!
Thy gift, I gave it to my menial slave
(Him it might suit, from poverty might save).
Had clear reflection e'er illum'd thy mind,
The bard had never damn'd thee to mankind—
No low'ring clouds had hover'd o'er my day;
Serene and mild had pass'd my evening ray—
Had not thy birth, polluted as thy soul,
Strove, tho' in vain, my genius to control.
Mortals attend—no low-born tyrant trust,
The truly great are to the Muses just—
The tree, whose native juices are defil'd,
No foliage shades, for ever rank and wild—
Tho' richest essence spreads its sweets around,
Tho' nurs'd and water'd on Elysian ground—
For ever wou'd its wither'd blossoms die,
And Art in vain her utmost efforts try—
Expect not, honour'd bards! tho' sweet your strain,
Plaudits, or trophies from the loose profane.

From tainted springs no lucid waters flow,
From the rank weed no roseate blossoms grow.
The slave of envy damns your tuneful lays,
Droops at your pow'rs, and sickens at your praise.

J. Champion.

KIYUMARS

Great deeds I sing! my guide recording time!
Imperial annals fill the song sublime
What chief invented first, the royal throne!
The rich Tiara, and the splendid zone?
'Twas *Kiyumars*! at whose auspicious birth
A smile expanded o'er the genial earth!
'Twas when yon sun was moving on his way
From Aries to the Lamb with brilliant ray.
On him fair worth and spotless honours beam,
Pure and unsullied as the limpid stream.
Tho' born midst hills, he felt an innate flame,
An humble chief, as then unknown to fame!
But when enthron'd, emerging into pow'r,
A grateful world confess'd the fav'ring hour!
For thirty years, the royal vest he wore,
He cloth'd the naked and he fed the poor!
As yon bright orb its borrow'd beam displays,
So beam'd the chief, with heav'n-reflected rays—
His form erect a manly lustre spread,
As the tall cypress rears its lofty head.
E'en at his sight the brute became serene,
And bow'd before his throne with placid mien.
So thinking mortals in some dome divine
Obedient bend before the awful shrine—
One son he had, pre-eminent in worth,
Like his fond Sire, a fav'rite of the earth!
Siamak was his name; alone the boy,
Each thought employ'd, and centr'd ev'ry joy.
As the young vines new life and vigour bring,
In him wou'd renovate the parent king.

A moment's absence wak'd the tender sigh,
And the fond tear stood trembling in his eye.
Fair peace attended, and a fav'ring gale
Thro' life auspicious, fill'd the swelling sail.
Rehmen alone, a demon damn'd to fame,
Breath'd hostile fury, and infernal flame.
Dire *Rehmen*'s soul teem'd with malignant rage,
To crush the monarch, and the rising age.
His daring son shook all a trembling world,
Fierce as the wolf, he wide destruction hurl'd.
Without reserve he every plan confest,
No fear he knew, no honour mov'd his breast.
The king intrepid dar'd the high alarm,
And, fatal courage! scorn'd the demon's arm.
Th' alarum spread, when in a vision'd dream,
A spirit aerial sung this mystic theme.
(Sweet as the voice, melodious as the lyre,
Resembling fairies whom the gods inspire.)
`Each artifice the demon tries in vain,
Vain his ambition, *Kiyumars* shall reign!'
On this *Siamak*, full of martial fire,
Call'd all his force, and brav'd the demon's ire.
A tiger's skin his manly limbs o'erspread,
No armour known, no helmets grac'd the head.
The hostile legions mov'd in firm array,
Front of the lines *Siamak* dares the fray.
The demon fought the youth, at fatal hour,
Both onward rush, yet such his mighty power,
Soon the brave youth lay welt'ring in his gore,
While the black fiend his beauteous body tore.
His dire associates, full of impious joy,
Of club and vest despoil the lovely boy.
The grief-struck army mourn'd—with rapid wing
Fame spread the story to the anguished king.
Long sorrow sate on ev'ry feeling breast,
Till heav'n by angels, thus its will exprest:
'Tears are of no avail! dispel thy grief,
Arm all your legions, rouse each warlike chief:

'Tis my decree. attack the fiend-like foe,
And bravely combat, blow revenge by blow.'
To heav'n the good old hero rais'd his eyes,
And grateful! blest the goodness of the skies!
Revenge alone now fill'd the Persian's breast,
Or day, or night, he knew no balmy rest.
On lov'd *Siamak*'s son his thoughts incline,
To teach in council, as in arms to shine.
Houshang his name, the king the youth addrest,
And thus declar'd the secrets of his breast:
'Ere long in arms my marshall's legions beam,
And hostile blood o'er yonder plain shall stream.
Thou must attend, a few short minutes o'er,
These aged limbs will seek another shore.
On me the aerial spirits gladly wait,
And e'en the brute creation guard my state.'
He spoke; in bright array his troops appear,
But feeble grown with age, he sought the rear.
High in the midst of the embattl'd host
Young Houshang stood, the royal *Persian*'s boast.
Onward each army rush'd with martial glow,
Revenge and empire dwell upon the blow.
Immortal vigour fir'd the *Persian* train,
And clouds of dust o'ershadow'd all the plain.
Proud and audacious! dauntful in the fight,
The demon rov'd, too confident of might.
His strokes on all re-echo, all engage,
As when the roaring lion hurls his rage.
The old king trembled, as he view'd the force
Of the dire demons mow their dreadful course;
'Twas then brave *Houshang* with undaunted might
Sought the young demon thro' the thickest fight.
They met, they fought, the hero's patriot glow
Gave force and vigour o'er the treach'rous foe.
Long was the combat, when the prince's arm
Struck the pale demon, trembling with alarm.
Then hurl'd him from his courser, as he fled,
And as he fell, he lopp'd his impious head.

With conquest in his arms the good old king
(The assassin of his son having felt the sting
Of death and of remorse) resign'd to fate
The splendid trappings of his earthly state.
A name alone remains, the greatest pow'r
Secures no mortal from the fatal hour.
Yet tho' his life in each exertion past,
Th' effect he knew not, when he breath'd his last.
Brave Kiyumars with patriotic sway
First taught th' untutor'd nations to obey.
A few short moments close this troubled scene,
And life's at best a nugatory dream!
How fruitless grief! how vain the plaintive sigh!
To stop pale death, or raise the dying eye!

J. Champion.

THE BIRTH OF ROSTAM

All nature teem'd with harmony divine,
And music floated o'er the sparkling wine.
Sindokht approach'd; 'Say when, illustrious queen,
Shall fair *Roudabeh* gild the splendid scene?'
Thus *Sam* addrest; and *Sindokht* leads the king
To the bright beauty, and the flow'ring spring.
There in the golden room, the chief amaz'd
With rapture at the moony fair one gaz'd.
Yet knew no language to express his praise,
Her charms transcendent, her illumin'd rays.
Mehrab advanc'd; in native rites he gave
The lovely princess to the warrior brave:
Gave nuptial presents; and then plac'd the pair,
Glowing with transport, on the regal chair.
Rapture sat smiling on the warrior's face;
He views his consort, blest with ev'ry grace.
This is the maid! his thoughts in secret roll,
The fascinating fairy of the soul!
In blushing glances she beheld her lord;
When all depart: and night with love's accord

Stole slyly on: when *Zal* the fair addrest,
And thus the raptures of his soul exprest
(*Roudabeh* seem'd a *Houri*, heav'nly bright!
And *Zal*'s bright eye appear'd the rays of light):
'Fate smiles at length propitiate on our flame,
And future bliss shall crown our spotless fame.'
With eager eye her scented musky hair,
Her form of elegance, her gracious air,
Dastan entranc'd beholds: he clasp'd her arms,
Prest her soft lips, all conscious of her charms!
How shall the bard the lover's joys impart?
Or paint their foncinecc, their united heart?
With the first dawn the happy warrior rose;
And bathing, pray'd, the solar planet glows.
When *Zal* returning to his beauteous bride,
The gallant *Mehrab*, glitt'ring by his side,
Amazing treasures gave: succeeding days
In festive joy on rich pavilions blaze.
The mighty warriors in the presence sate;
Till *Za1* retiring to *Sistan*'s state,
With his fair bride, and *Sindokht* the divine;
When Sam, delighted with his warlike line,
Bestow'd the kingdom on his blooming heirs,
To *Backsher* and *Kergerseran* repairs.
Many a day in elevated joy
The lovers pass, and all their hours employ.
When fair *Roudabeh* gave the blissful sign,
To make *Zal* parent of a beauteous line.
But soon alas! ill health her frame invades;
The roses fly, and all her beauty fades.
'Why, why so wan?' the tender mother cri'd,
'Nor day or night I rest,' the queen repli'd;
'The fear of death alarms my anxious care,
I dread the mighty burden that I bear.'
Yet soft repose her pensive mind restores,
The pow'r omniscient pious *Zal* implores.
When on a morn the fainting princess pale
Sinks on the ground, and all her senses fail.

Pale *Sindokht* heard the news, the plaintive fair,
Wild with her grief rends her dishevell'd hair.
Those jetty tresses where the rich perfume
Of playful odours scents the musky room.
The mournful tale to *Dastan* was convey'd,
That the tall cypress wither'd and decay'd.
Now near *Roudabeh*'s pillow dew'd in tears,
The yellow *Zal* with anguish'd grief appears,
Torn is his soul by frantic sorrows prest:
He clasps his hands and beats his swol'n breast;
The faithful servants in their cares unite,
Run round their queen, a miserable sight!
Much *Zal* revolves, by adverse fate opprest,
Tho' sapient contemplation leads to rest,
When recollective of the *Simorgh*'s strain,
The promis'd feather to relieve his pain.
O'er all his face the smile of hope is seen,
He speaks his thoughts to the distracted queen.
The kettle brought, high blaz'd the mounting flame,
Burnt was the feather; in an instant came
The shrouded *Simorgh* in a cloud array'd,
Where all the lustre of a gem's display'd.
Such gems as glitter radiant on the breast;
To *Zal* she came with happy omens blest.
She prais'd the chief, for him her fervent pray'rs,
And *Zal* to her his gratitude declares.
The *Simorgh* spoke: 'Why grieves the warlike chief?
Why are the lion's eyes bedew'd in grief?
From this fair cypress, from thy moony dame,
Shall spring a hero of immortal fame,
When the brave warrior views his manly form,
His mighty club, and the resistless storm,
prostrate he falls; his voice shall spread alarm,
And ev'ry warrior tremble at his arm.
Gay at the banquet he like *Sam* will shine,
A martial lion in th' embattled line;
In stature the tall cypress will he prove,
In strength the chief an elephant will move;

Two miles a brick the future chief will throw,
Victor of worlds! triumphant o'er the foe!
By God's high favour will his glories blaze,
And *Zal* will triumph in his glorious rays.
Bring the sharp knife, a skilful artist chuse,
Then thro' the lady's veins bright wine infuse,
Do thou attend: extract the child and place
The future hero in a wooden case.
Then cut the hollow in the lady's side;
All pain shall cease, and ev'ry care subside.
Then sew th' incision, tranquillize your mind,
Dread no alarm, be ev'ry fear resign'd.
Pound milk and musk with grass, be these convey'd,
And dri'd the three together in the shade.
To the incision thou this salve apply,
Soon it will heal, and charm thy anxious eye.
Then take this feather, rub it o'er the wound:
The shadow of my glory is renown'd!
Do thou rejoice, high triumph at my strain,
And in the presence of the king remain.
'Twas he who gave thee this imperial dame,
To raise thy splendour, and adorn thy name.
Let not thy heart with fearful anguish shoot,
Thy faithful branches are surcharg'd with fruit.'
She spoke, and from her wing a feather throws;
Exalted *Zal* with grateful fervour glows:
He takes the feather, when the *Simorgh* flies;
And *Zal* submiss the remedy applies.
Amazing operation! wondrous deed!
One world beholds it, all their senses bleed.
The purple drops fell from the eyes of *Sin*,
Oh! strange idea! from the parent queen,
From her fair side to take th' infant child;
A skilful artist waits, with tremor wild,
The queen the beauty drinks the flowing bowl;
Cut is the side, no pain opprest her soul.
He turn'd the infant's head, and when he saw
The wondrous birth, above all nature's law,

The youthful lion charm'd the gazing sight,
Of lofty stature, eminently bright!
All stood amaz'd, no mortal ever knew
An infant, like the elephant in view.
For days and nights th' intoxicated queen
Was lost in slumber, ev'ry sense serene.
They sew th' incision, and the order'd balm
Healing all pain, produc'd a tranquil calm.
When she awoke, rich presents she bestow'd;
To him, the lord of all her praises flow'd.
They bring the child, exalt it to the skies;
The queen arose, and opes her radiant eyes;
She sees the burthen from her womb remov'd,
And eyes the manly child, by all approv'd.
The lovely boy whose skin was heav'nly fair,
Roseate his cheeks, and black his infant hair.
His breast like jessamine; the boy appears,
As if two summers saw his infant years.
Thus hyacinths and tulips sweetly rise,
And floreate gardens beautify the skies.
Roudabeh smil'd, and in her son she view'd
Majestic grace, and thus the theme pursu'd.
'Clos'd are my labours.' And from this the name
Of *Rostam* rose, the glorious chief of fame!
Zal and *Roudabeh* glow'd with raptur'd joy,
Conven'd the sage; in semblance of the boy,
They form'd a figure of a child of silk,
Who ne'er had tasted yet the parent's milk.
Stuff'd with the weasel's soft and furry hair,
And on the cheek was *Venus* painted fair,
All brilliant with the sun. And on the arm
A dreadful snake; the lion's claws alarm
Depicted on his hand, in which appear'd
A waving standard; while the other rear'd
A bridle high; on a dun horse they place,
And lead the image with the lion's grace.
(Throngs of attendants crowd around the horse,
Large gifts were thrown, in honour of the course.)

The convoy of age, Mohammad-Ali Zaviyeh, 48×72 cm., 1973

A party, Mohammad-Ali Zaviyeh, 38×57 cm., 1970

This martial figure was to *Zal* convey'd,
Young *Rostam*'s image borne in great parade.
A jubilee in ev'ry garden blaz'd,
Hence to *Kabol* the voice of joy was rais'd.
While wine and music flow'd on ev'ry plain,
And jovial crowds unite their blissful strain.
Mehrab enraptur'd the vast gift bestows,
And the poor mendicant forgets his woes.
Thro' *Zabol* music aids the vocal train,
Yet still more num'rous thro' *Sistan*'s reign
Each tongue of *Rostam* with his praise resounds,
The roads were crowded from the distant bounds.
The gazing travellers, the way along,
In numbers meet, as when the village throng
To market crowd; nor did the lower class
In numbers the nobility surpass.
As interwoven threads the crowds unite,
Before great *Sam*, the image in his sight,
The grand procession moves; astonish'd *Sam*
Eyes the fine figure, and with rapture warm:
'Behold the semblance of myself,' he cries.
'This boy will one day reach the azure skies,
And stride along the earth.' Rich gifts he gave,
High as the image did his presents wave
The sounding drums beat high; far blazing light
Illuminates the plain, refulgent, bright!
The king commands that *Sugser*, dog-like town!
And fierce *Mazandaran*, the victor's crown,
Shou'd blaze with light; while gifts profusely gay
To skilful dancers, and the minstrel's lay,
The warrior gave: so splendid was the feast,
The moon descended with the beaming east.
Now *Sam* to *Zal* replies; and in the line
His soul was painted; to the pow'r divine
High flow'd his plaudits, for his blissful days:
Next to his son deserving all his praise.
'The image I have seen, there greatly springs
The force of heroes and the fame of kings.'

(He now commands to keep the boy sublime,
Exempt from danger, or the varying clime.)
'For such a child in secret have I pray'd;
For such a child implor'd celestial aid.
While flow'd my tide of life I might behold
From thee an offspring, like his grandsire bold.
Now that he lives, what more can I desire;
The heir of glory like his martial sire.'
Swift as the wind the letter was convey'd
To joyful *Zal*, whose eye such bliss display'd
At the glad strain, that his elated soul
Glow'd thro' his frame in one tumultuous roll.
Transport to transport bore his mind on high,
His feet on earth, his head above the sky.
Ten nurses cherish'd the amazing youth;
The principle of lions, manly truth,
And manly strength, first mark'd his infant years.
When milk no more the mighty *Rostam* cheers,
With bread the mighty boy five sheep devours,
Mankind astonish'd ey'd his wond'rous pow'rs.
Eight years had pass'd, illustrious beam'd his fire,
As the tall cypress rising in a spire.
Resembling a bright star, which all the train
With wonder views, on the celestial plain.
In mien and stature like the hero *Sam*,
In wisdom, intellect, and mighty form.
Zal was his tutor in the letter'd rays,
That fortune might adorn his future days.
When *Sam* the brave, resistless in his course,
Who guides thro' warring fields his furious horse,
First heard that *Rostam* like a lion grew,
That such a child no mortal ever knew,
Such strength, such courage, wonderful to view!
To clasp the lion-boy high beat his veins,
He leaves a leader of his martial trains;
And with the chosen few his march begun,
To *Zabol*'s realms, and his immortal son.

When *Zal* was told th' intention of his sire,
The drums proclaim'd it, and with warlike fire
The num'rous forces blacken all the ground,
One plain of ebony appears around.
Now *Mehrab*, *Zal*, resolve to meet the king,
The signal giv'n, they the march begin.
On ev'ry side the joyful shouts began,
Thro' armies eager all the tumult ran.
Thus mountains rising in alternate spires
Are lost to view while one to heav'n aspires.
Whole groves of shields of various hues unite,
The neighing steeds, and elephants of might,
Resound for many a mile. One royal strong
Blaz'd with a golden howdah 'bove the throng.
On it was plac'd bright *Zal*'s immortal son
(The prize of glory, and of love he won),
Whose limbs and stature the tall cypress grac'd,
Crowns on his head, and zones around his waist.
High blaz'd his shield, and in his hand appear
The weighty jav'lin, and the pond'rous spear.
Mehrab and *Zal* precede the wondrous child:
Like indigo the dust the chiefs defil'd.
But *Rostam*'s face thro' clouds appear'd more bright,
Like the gay planet in meridian height.
When *Sam* from far the mighty warrior shines,
The troops were rang'd in two embattl'd lines,
Mehrab and *Zal* alight; the old and young
Swift from their steeds with awful reverence sprung.
They bow their heads obedient to the ground,
The praise of *Sam* re-echoes all around.
Not with more colour beams the blushing rose,
Than *Sam* at viewing the young hero glows.
The elephant approach'd, the warrior views
The mighty child, and thus the strain pursues:
'Blest be thy days! for ever live in fame!
Thou valiant youth! the glory of our name!
Thou son of *Zal*! thou king of high renown!
Oh! thou dost merit an imperial crown!

Thou splendid moon! be this thy mortal praise!
Like *Sam* thy glories, thou thyself will raise!'
Rostam submissive how'd, and strange to tell,
His grandsire's fame thus eloquently fell
From his young voice; and to the youth around
Thus did his strain, and thus the praise resound:
'For ever live, thou hero of the earth!
Thy branch am I, to thee I owe my birth.
Thou art the tree, from whose illustrious root
Grows the straight branch, and th' unerring shoot.
For ever and for ever may'st thou reign!
Thence flows my transports thro' the thrilling vein.
My time to ease, to sloth, shall never yield;
Give me the courser, helmet, and the shield!
The spear, the javelin, I will dart along,
And break like thunder o'er the hostile throng.
Thy foes shall prostrate at thy footsteps bend,
Like thine my image and my fame ascend!'

J. Champion.

SOHRAB IS BORN

One watch had passed, and still sweet slumber shed
Its magic power around the hero's head–
When forth *Tahmineh* came –a damsel held
An amber taper, which the gloom dispelled,
And near his pillow stood; in beauty bright,
The monarch's daughter struck his wondering sight.
Clear as the moon, in glowing charms arrayed,
Her winning eyes the light of heaven displayed;
Her cypress form entranced the gazer's view,
Her waving curls the heart, resistless, drew,
Her eyebrows like the Archer's bended bow;
Her ringlets, snares; her cheek, the rose's glow,
Mixed with the lily –from her ear-tips hung
Rings rich and glittering, star –like; and her tongue,
And lips, all sugared sweetness –pearls the while
Sparkled within a mouth formed to beguile.

Her presence dimmed the stars, and breathing round
Fragrance and joy, she scarcely touched the ground,
So light her step, so graceful-every part
Perfect, and suited to her spotless heart.
Rostam, surprised, the gentle maid addressed,
And asked what lovely stranger broke his rest.
'What is thy name?' he said–'what dost thou seek
Amidst the gloom of night? Fair vision, speak!'
'O thou,' she softly sigh'd, 'of matchless fame!
With pity hear, Tahmineh is my name!
The pangs of love my anxious heart employ,
And flattering promise long-expected joy;
No curious eye has yet these features seen,
My voice unheard, beyond the sacred screen.
How often have I listened with amaze
To thy great deeds, enamoured of thy praise;
How oft from every tongue I've heard the strain,
And thought of thee –and sighed, and sighed again.
The ravenous eagle, hovering o'er his prey,
Starts at thy gleaming sword and flies away:
Thou art the slayer of the Demon brood,
And the fierce monsters of the echoing wood.
Where'er thy mace is seen, shrink back the bold,
Thy javelin's flash all tremble to behold.
Enchanted with the stories of thy fame,
My fluttering heart responded to thy name;
And whilst their magic influence I felt,
In prayer for thee devotedly I knelt;
And fervent vowed, thus powerful glory charms,
No other spouse should bless my longing arms.
Indulgent heaven propitious to my prayer
Now brings thee hither to reward my care.
Turan's dominions thou hast sought, alone,
By night, in darkness–thou, the mighty one!
Oh claim my hand, and grant my soul's desire;
Ask me in marriage of my royal sire;
Perhaps a boy our wedded love may crown,
Whose strength like thine may gain the world's renown.

Nay more—for Samengan will keep my word—
Rakhsh to thee again shall be restored.'
The damsel thus her ardent thought expressed,
And Rostam's heart beat joyous in his breast,
Hearing her passion-not a word was lost,
And Rakhsh safe, by him still valued most;
He called her near; with graceful step she came,
And marked with throbbing pulse his kindled flame.
And now a Mubid, from the Champion-knight,
Requests the royal sanction to the rite;
O'erjoyed, the king the honoured suit approves,
O'erjoyed to bless the doting child he loves,
And happier still, in showering smiles around,
To be allied to warrior so renowned.
When the delighted father, doubly blest,
Resigned his daughter to his glorious guest,
The people shared the gladness which it gave,
The union of the beauteous and the brave.
To grace their nuptial day—both old and young
The hymeneal gratulations sung:
'May this young moon bring happiness and joy,
And every source of enmity destroy.'
The marriage-bower received the happy pair,
And love and transport shower'd their blessings there.
Ere from his lofty sphere the morn had thrown
His glittering radiance, and in splendour shone,
The mindful Champion, from his sinewy arm,
His bracelet drew, the soul-ennobling charm; And,
as he held the wondrous gift with pride,
He thus address'd his love-devoted bride:
'Take this,' he said, 'and if, by gracious heaven,
A daughter for thy solace should be given,
Let it among her ringlets be displayed,
And joy and honour will await the maid;
But should kind Fate increase the nuptial-joy,
And make thee mother of a blooming boy,
Around his arm this magic bracelet bind,
To fire with virtuous deeds his ripening mind;

The strength of Sam will nerve his manly form,
In temper mild, in valour like the storm;
His not the dastard fate to shrink, or turn
From where the lions of the battle burn;
To him the soaring eagle from the sky
Will stoop, the bravest yield to him, or fly;
Thus shall his bright career imperious claim
The well-won honours of immortal fame!'
Ardent he said, and kissed her eyes and face,
And lingering held her in a fond embrace.

When the bright sun his radiant brow displayed,
And earth in all its loveliest hues arrayed,
The Champion rose to leave his spouse's side,
The warm affections of his weeping bride.
For her too soon the wingéd moments flew,
Too soon, alas! the parting hour she knew;
Clasped in his arms, with many a streaming tear
She tried, in vain, to win his deafen'd ear;
Still tried, ah fruitless struggle! to impart
The swelling anguish of her bursting heart.

The father now with gratulations due
Rostam approaches, and displays to view
The fiery war-horse—welcome as the light
Of heaven, to one immersed in deepest night,
The Champion, wild with joy, fits on the rein,
And girds the saddle on his back again;
Then mounts, and leaving sire and wife behind,
Onward to Sistan rushes like the wind.

But when returned to Zabol's friendly shade,
None knew what joys the Warrior had delayed;
Still, fond remembrance, with endearing thought,
Oft to his mind the scene of rapture brought.

When nine slow-circling months had roll'd away,
Sweet-smiling pleasure hailed the brightening day—
A wondrous boy Tahmineh's tears suppressed,
And lull'd the sorrows of her heart to rest;
To him, predestined to be great and brave,
The name Sohrab his tender mother gave;

And as he grew, amazed, the gathering throng
View'd his large limbs, his sinews firm and strong;
His infant years no soft endearment claimed:
Athletic sports his eager soul inflamed;
Broad at the chest and taper round the loins,
Where to the rising hip the body joins;
Hunter and wrestler; and so great his speed,
He could o'ertake, and hold the swiftest steed.
His noble aspect, and majestic grace,
Betrayed the offspring of a glorious race.
How, with a mother's ever-anxious love,
Still to retain him near her heart she strove!
For when the father's fond inquiry came,
Cautious, she still concealed his birth and name,
And feign'd a daughter born, the evil fraught
With misery to avert—but vain the thought;
Not many years had passed, with downy flight,
Ere he, Tahmineh's wonder and delight,
With glistening eye, and youthful ardour warm,
Filled her foreboding bosom with alarm.
'Oh now relieve my heart!' he said, 'declare
From whom I sprang and breathe the vital air.
Since, from my childhood I have ever been
Amidst my playmates of superior mien;
Should friend or foe demand my father's name,
Let not my silence testify my shame!
If still concealed, you falter, still delay,
A mother's blood shall wash the crime away.'

'This wrath forgo,' the mother answering cried,
'And joyful hear to whom thou art allied.
A glorious line precedes thy destined birth,
The mightiest heroes of the sons of earth.
The deeds of Sam remotest realms admire,
And Zal, and Rostam thy illustrious sire!'

In private, then, she Rostam's letter placed
Before his view, and brought with eager haste
Three sparkling rubies, wedges three of gold,
From Persia sent—'Behold,' she said, 'behold

Thy father's gifts, will these thy doubts remove,
The costly pledges of paternal love!
Behold this bracelet charm, of sovereign power
To baffle fate in danger's awful hour;
But thou must still the perilous secret keep,
Nor ask the harvest of renown to reap;
For when, by this peculiar signet known,
Thy glorious father shall demand his son,
Doomed from her only joy in life to part,
Oh think what pangs will rend thy mother's heart!—
Seek not the fame which only teems with woe;
Afrasiab is Rostam's deadliest foe!
And if by him discovered, him I dread,
Revenge will fall upon thy guiltless head.'
The youth replied: `In vain thy sighs and tears,
The secret breathes and mocks thy idle fears.
No human power can fate's decrees control,
Or check the kindled ardour of my soul.
Then why from me the bursting truth conceal?
My father's foes even now my vengeance feel;
Even now in wrath my native legions rise,
And sounds of desolation strike the skies;
Kavous himself, hurled from his ivory throne,
Shall yield to Rostam the imperial crown,
And thou, my mother, still in triumph seen,
Of lovely Persia hailed the honoured queen!
Then shall Turan unite beneath my band,
And drive this proud oppressor from the land!
Father and Son, in virtuous league combined,
No savage despot shall enslave mankind;
When Sun and Moon o'er heaven refulgent blaze,
Shall little Stars obtrude their feeble rays?'
    He paused, and then: 'O mother, I must now
My father seek, and see his lofty brow;
Be mine a horse, such as a prince demands,
Fit for the dusty field, a warrior's hands;
Strong as an elephant his form should be,
And chested like the stag, in motion free,

And swift as bird, or fish; it would disgrace
A warrior bold on foot to show his face.'
The mother, seeing how his heart was bent,
His day-star rising in the firmament,
Commands the stables to be searched to find
Among the steeds one suited to his mind;
Pressing their backs he tries their strength and nerve,
Bent double to the ground their bellies curve;
Not one, from neighbouring plain and mountain brought,
Equals the wish with which his soul is fraught;
Fruitless on every side he anxious turns,
Fruitless, his brain with wild impatience burns,
But when at length they bring the destined steed,
From Rakhsh bred, of lightning's wingéd speed,
Fleet, as the arrow from the bow-string flies,
Fleet, as the eagle darting through the skies,
Rejoiced he springs, and, with a nimble bound,
Vaults in his seat, and wheels the courser round;
'With such a horse—thus mounted, what remains?
Kavous, the Persian King, no longer reigns!'
High flushed he speaks —with youthful pride elate,
Eager to crush the Monarch's glittering state;
He grasps his javelin with a hero's might,
And pants with ardour for the field of fight.

J. Atkinson.

ROSTAM SLAYS SOHRAB

Rostam, meanwhile, the thickening tumult hears
And in his heart, untouched by human fears,
Says: 'What is this, that feeling seems to stun!
This battle must be led by Ahriman,
The awful day of doom must have begun.'
In haste he arms, and mounts his bounding steed,
The growing rage demands redoubled speed;
The leopard's skin he o'er his shoulders throws,
The regal girdle round his middle glows.
High wave his glorious banners; broad revealed,
The pictured dragons glare along the field,

Borne by Zuara. When, surprised, he views
Sohrab, endued with ample breast and thews,
Like Sam Suwar, he beckons him apart;
The youth advances with a gallant heart,
Willing to prove his adversary's might,
By single combat to decide the fight;
And eagerly: 'Together brought,' he cries,
'Remote from us be foemen, and allies,
And though at once by either host surveyed,
Ours be the strife which asks no mortal aid.'
    Rostam, considerate, view'd him o'er and o'er,
So wondrous graceful was the form he bore,
And frankly said: 'Experience flows with age,
And many a foe has felt my conquering rage;
Much have I seen, superior strength and art
Have borne my spear thro' many a demon's heart;
Only behold me on the battle plain,
Wait till thou see'st this hand the war sustain,
And if on thee should changeful fortune smile,
Thou needst not fear the monster of the Nile!
But soft compassion melts my soul to save
A youth so blooming with a mind so brave!'
    The generous speech Sohrab attentive heard,
His heart expanding glowed at every word:
'One question answer, and in answering show
That truth should ever from a warrior flow:
Art thou not Rostam, whose exploits sublime
Endear his name thro' every distant clime?'
    'I boast no station of exalted birth,
No proud pretensions to distinguished worth;
To him inferior, no such powers are mine,
No offspring I of Nirum's glorious line!'
    The prompt denial dampt his filial joy,
All hope at once forsook the Warrior-boy,
His opening day of pleasure, and the bloom
Of cherished life, immersed in shadowy gloom.
Perplexed with what his mother's words implied—
A narrow space is now prepared, aside,

For single combat. With disdainful glance
Each boldly shakes his death-devoting lance,
And rushes forward to the dubious fight;
Thoughts high and brave their burning souls excite;
Now sword to sword; continuous strokes resound,
Till glittering fragments strew the dusty ground.
Each grasps his massive club with added force,
The folding mail is rent from either horse;
It seemed as if the fearful day of doom
Had, clothed in all its withering terrors, come.
Their shattered corslets yield defence no more—
At length they breathe, defiled with dust and gore;
Their gasping throats with parching thirst are dry,
Gloomy and fierce they roll the lowering eye,
And frown defiance. Son and Father driven
To mortal strife! are these the ways of Heaven?
The various swarms which boundless ocean breeds,
The countless tribes which crop the flowery meads,
All know their kind, but hapless man alone
Has no instinctive feeling for his own!
Compell'd to pause, by every eye surveyed,
Rostam, with shame, his wearied strength betrayed;
Foil'd by a youth in battle's mid career,
His groaning spirit almost sunk with fear;
Recovering strength, again they fiercely meet;
Again they struggle with redoubled heat;
With bended bows they furious now contend;
And feather'd shafts in rattling showers descend;
Thick as autumnal leaves they strew the plain,
Harmless their points, and all their fury vain.
And now they seize each other's girdle-band;
Rostam, who, if he moved his iron hand,
Could shake a mountain, and to whom a rock
Seemed soft as wax, tried, with one mighty stroke,
To send him thundering from his fiery steed,
But Fate forbids the gallant youth should bleed;
Finding his wonted nerves relaxed, amazed,
That hand he drops which never had been raised

Uncrowned with victory, even when demons fought,
And pauses, wildered with despairing thought.
Sohrab again springs with terrific grace,
And lifts, from saddle-bow, his ponderous mace;
With gather'd strength the quick-descending blow
Wounds in its fall, and stuns the unwary foe;
Then thus contemptuous: 'All thy power is gone;
Thy charger's strength exhausted as thy own;
Thy bleeding wounds with pity I behold;
Oh seek no more the combat of the bold!'
    Rostam to this reproach made no reply,
But stood confused—meanwhile, tumultuously
The legions closed; with soul-appalling force
Troop rushed on troop, o'erwhelming man and horse;
Sohrab, incensed, the Persian host engaged,
Furious along the scattered lines he raged;
Fierce as a wolf he rode on every side,
The thirsty earth with streaming gore was dyed.
Midst the Turanians, then, the Champion sped,
And like a tiger heaped the fields with dead.
But when the Monarch's danger struck his thought,
Returning swift, the stripling youth he sought;
Grieved to the soul, the mighty Champion view'd
His hands and mail with Persian blood imbrued;
And thus exclaimed with lion-voice: 'Oh say,
Why with the Persians dost thou war to-day?
Why not with me alone decide the fight,
Thou'rt like a wolf that seek'st the fold by night.'
    To this Sohrab his proud assent expressed—
And Rostam, answering, thus the youth addressed:
'Night-shadows now are thickening o'er the plain,
The morrow's sun must see our strife again;
In wrestling let us then exert our might!'
He said, and eve's last glimmer sunk in night.
    Thus as the skies a deeper gloom displayed,
The stripling's life was hastening into shade!
    The gallant heroes to their tents retired,
The sweets of rest their wearied limbs required:

Sohrab, delighted with his brave career,
Describes the fight in Houman's anxious ear:
Tells how he forced unnumbered Chiefs to yield,
And stood himself the victor of the field!
'But let the morrow's dawn,' he cried, 'arrive,
And not one Persian shall the day survive;
Meanwhile let wine its strengthening balm impart
And add new zeal to every drooping heart.'
The valiant Giw with Rostam pondering stood,
And, sad, recalled the scene of death and blood;
Grief and amazement heaved the frequent sigh,
And almost froze the crimson current dry.
Rostam, oppressed by Giw's desponding thought,
Amidst his Chiefs the mournful Monarch sought;
To him he told Sohrab's tremendous sway,
The dire misfortunes of this luckless day;
Told with what grasping force he tried, in vain,
To hurl the wondrous stripling to the plain:
'The whispering zephyr might as well aspire
To shake a mountain –such his strength and fire.
But night came on –and, by agreement, we
Must meet again to-morrow –who shall be
Victorious, Heaven knows only –for by Heaven
Victory or death to man is ever given.'
This said, the King, o'erwhelmed in deep despair,
Passed the dread night in agony and prayer.
    The Champion, silent, joined his bands at rest,
And spurned at length despondence from his breast;
Removed from all, he cheered Zuara's heart,
And nerved his soul to bear a trying part:
'Ere early morning gilds the ethereal plain,
in martial order range my warrior-train;
And when I meet in all his glorious pride
This valiant Turk whom late my rage defied,
Should fortune's smiles my arduous task requite,
Bring them to share the triumph of my might;
But should success the stripling's arm attend,
And dire defeat and death my glories end,

To their loved homes my brave associates guide;
Let bowery Zabol all their sorrows hide—
Comfort my venerable father's heart;
In gentlest words my heavy fate impart.
The dreadful tidings to my mother bear,
And soothe her anguish with the tenderest care;
Say, that the will of righteous Heaven decreed
That thus in arms her mighty son should bleed.
Enough of fame my various toils acquired
When warring demons, bathed in blood, expired.
Were life prolonged a thousand lingering years,
Death comes at last and ends our mortal fears;
Garshasp, and Sam, and Nariman, the best
And bravest heroes who have ever blest
This fleeting world, were not endued with power
To stay the march of fate one single hour;
The world for them possessed no fixed abode,
The path to death's cold regions must be trod;
Then why lament the doom ordained for all?
Thus Jamshid fell, and thus must Rostam fall.'

When the bright dawn proclaimed the rising day,
The warriors armed, impatient of delay;
But first Sohrab, his proud confederate nigh,
Thus wistful spoke, as swelled the boding sigh
`Now mark my great antagonist in arms!
His noble form my filial bosom warms;
My mother's tokens shine conspicuous here,
And all the proofs my heart demands appear;
Sure this is Rostam, whom my eyes engage!
Shall I, Oh grief! provoke my Father's rage?
Offended Nature then would curse my name,
And shuddering nations echo with my shame.'
He ceased, then Houman: 'Vain, fantastic thought;
Oft have I been where Persia's Champion fought;
And thou hast heard what wonders he performed,
When, in his prime, Mazandaran was stormed;
That horse resembles Rostam's, it is true,
But not so strong, nor beautiful to view.'

Sohrab now buckles on his war-attire,
His heart all softness, and his brain all fire;
Around his lips such smiles benignant played,
He seemed to greet a friend, as thus he said:
'Here let us sit together on the plain,
Here social sit, and from the fight refrain;
Ask we from heaven forgiveness of the past,
And bind our souls in friendship that may last;
Ours be the feast –let us be warm and free,
For powerful instinct draws me still to thee;
Fain would my heart in bland affection join,
Then let thy generous ardour equal mine;
And kindly say, with whom I now contend–
What name distinguished boasts my warrior-friend!
Thy name unfit for champion brave to hide,
Thy name so long, long sought, and still denied;
Say, art thou Rostam, whom I burn to know?
Ingenuous say, and cease to be my foe!'
Sternly the mighty Champion cried: 'Away–
Hence with thy wiles –now practised to delay;
The promised struggle, resolute, I claim,
Then cease to move me to an act of shame.
Sohrab rejoined: 'Old man! thou wilt not hear
The words of prudence uttered in thine ear;
Then, Heaven! look on.'
Preparing for the shock,
Each binds his charger to a neighbouring rock;
And girds his loins, and rubs his wrists, and tries
Their suppleness and force, with angry eyes;
And now they meet –now rise, and now ascend,
And strong and fierce their sinewy arms extend;
Wrestling with all their strength they grasp and strain,
And blood and sweat flow copious on the plain;
Like raging elephants they furious close;
Commutual wounds are given, and wrenching blows.
Sohrab now claps his hands, and forward springs
Impatiently, and round the Champion clings;

The Blue Dome assembly, Mohammad Tajvidi, 66×97 cm., 1970

The General Office of Bonyad Museums

The lute player, Naser Oweisi, 82×130 cm., 1967

Seizes his girdle-belt, with power to tear
The very earth asunder; in despair
Rostam, defeated, feels his nerves give way,
And thundering falls. Sohrab bestrides his prey:
Grim as the lion, prowling through the wood,
Upon a wild ass springs, and pants for blood.
His lifted sword had lopt the gory head,
But Rostam, quick, with crafty ardour said:
'One moment, hold! what, are our laws unknown?
A Chief may fight till he is twice o'erthrown;
The second fall, his recreant blood is spilt;
These are our laws, avoid the menaced guilt.
Proud of his strength, and easily deceived,
The wondering youth the artful tale believed;
Released his prey, and, wild as wind or wave,
Neglecting all the prudence of the brave,
Turned from the place, nor once the strife renewed,
But bounded o'er the plain and other cares pursued,
As if all memory of the war had died,
All thoughts of him with whom his strength was tried.
Houman confounded at the stripling's stay,
Went forth, and heard the fortune of the day;
Amazed to find the mighty Rostam freed,
With deepest grief he wailed the luckless deed.
'What! loose a raging lion from the snare,
And let him growling hasten to his lair?
Bethink thee well; in war, from this unwise,
This thoughtless act what countless woes may rise;
Never again suspend the final blow,
Nor trust the seeming weakness of a foe!
'Hence with complaint,' the dauntless youth replied,
'To-morrow's contest shall his fate decide.'
When Rostam was released, in altered mood
He sought the coolness of the murmuring flood;
There quenched his thirst; and bathed his limbs, and prayed,
Beseeching Heaven to yield its strengthening aid.
His pious prayer indulgent Heaven approved,
And growing strength through all his sinews moved;

Such as erewhile his towering structure knew,
When his bold arm unconquered demons slew.
Yet in his mien no confidence appeared,
No ardent hope his wounded spirits cheered.
   Again they met. A glow of youthful grace
Diffused its radiance o'er the stripling's face,
And when he saw in renovated guise
The foe so lately mastered, with surprise
He cried: 'What! rescued from my power, again
Dost thou confront me on the battle plain?
Or dost thou, wearied, draw thy vital breath
And seek, from warrior bold, the shaft of death?
Truth has no charms for thee, old man; even now
Some further cheat may lurk upon thy brow;
Twice have I shewn thee mercy, twice thy age
Hath been thy safety—twice it soothed my rage.'
Then mild the Champion: 'Youth is proud and vain!
The idle boast a warrior would disdain;
This aged arm perhaps may yet control
The wanton fury that inflames thy soul!'
   Again, dismounting, each the other viewed
With sullen glance, and swift the fight renewed;
Clenched front to front, again they tug and bend,
Twist their broad limbs as every nerve would rend;
With rage convulsive Rostam grasps him round;
Bends his strong back, and hurls him to the ground;
Him, who had deemed the triumph all his own;
But dubious of his power to keep him down,
Like lightning quick he gives the deadly thrust,
And spurns the Stripling weltering in the dust—
Thus as his blood that shining steel imbrues,
Thine too shall flow, when Destiny pursues;
For when she marks the victim of her power,
A thousand daggers speed the dying hour.
Writhing in pain Sohrab in murmurs sighed—
And thus to Rostam: 'Vaunt not, in thy pride;
Upon myself this sorrow have I brought,
Thou but the instrument of fate —which wrought

My downfall; thou art guiltless —guiltless quite;
Oh! had I seen my father in the fight,
My glorious father! Life will soon be o'er,
And his great deeds enchant my soul no more!
Of him my mother gave the mark and sign,
For him I sought, and what an end is mine!
My only wish on earth, my constant sigh,
Him to behold, and with that wish I die.
But hope not to elude his piercing sight,
In vain for thee the deepest glooms of night;
Couldst thou through Ocean's depths for refuge fly,
Or midst the star-beams track the upper sky!
Rostam, with vengeance armed, will reach thee there,
His soul the prey of anguish and despair.'
    An icy horror chills the Champion's heart,
His brain whirls round with agonizing smart;
O'er his wan cheek no gushing sorrows flow,.
Senseless he sinks beneath the weight of woe;
Relieved at length, with frenzied look he cries:
'Prove thou art mine, confirm my doubting eyes!
For I am Rostam!' Piercing was the groan
Which burst from his torn heart—as wild and lone
He gazed upon him. Dire amazement shook
The dying youth, and mournful thus he spoke:
'If thou art Rostam, cruel is thy part,
No warmth paternal seems to fill thy heart;
Else hadst thou known me when, with strong desire.
I fondly claimed thee for my valiant sire;
Now from my body strip the shining mail,
Untie these bands, ere life and feeling fail;
And on my arm the direful proof behold!
Thy sacred bracelet of refulgent gold!
When the loud brazen drums were heard afar,
And, echoing round, proclaimed the pending war,
Whilst parting, tears my mother's eyes o'erflowed;
This mystic gift her bursting heart bestowed:
"Take this," she said, "thy father's token wear,
And promised glory will reward thy care."

The hour is come, but fraught with bitterest woe;
We meet in blood to wail the fatal blow.'
  The loosened mail unfolds the bracelet bright,
Unhappy gift! to Rostam's wildered sight;
Prostrate he falls —'By my unnatural hand,
My son, my son is slain—and from the land
Uprooted.' Frantic, in the dust his hair
He rends in agony and deep despair;
The western sun had disappeared in gloom,
And still the Champion wept his cruel doom;
His wondering legions marked the long delay,
And, seeing Rakhsh riderless astray,
The rumour quick to Persia's Monarch spread,
And there described the mighty Rostam dead.
Kavous, alarmed, the fatal tidings hears;
His bosom quivers with increasing fears.
'Speed, speed, and see what has befallen to-day
To cause these groans and tears—what fatal fray!
If he be lost, if breathless on the ground,
And this young warrior with the conquest crowned—
Then must I, humbled, from my kingdom torn,
Wander like Jamshid, through the world forlorn.'
  The army roused, rushed o'er the dusty plain,
Urged by the Monarch to revenge the slain;
Wild consternation saddened every face,
Tus winged with horror sought the fatal place,
And there beheld the agonizing sight—
The murderous end of that unnatural fight.
Sohrab, still breathing, hears the shrill alarms,
His gentle speech suspends the clang of arms:
'My light of life now fluttering sinks in shade,
Let vengeance sleep, and peaceful vows be made.
Beseech the King to spare —this Tartar host,
For they are guiltless, all to them is lost;
I led them on, their souls with glory fired,
While mad ambition all my thoughts inspired.
In search of thee, the world before my eyes,
War was my choice, and thou the sacred prize;

With thee, my sire! in virtuous league combined,
No tyrant King should persecute mankind.
That hope is past—the storm has ceased to rave—
My ripening honours wither in the grave;
Then let no vengeance on my comrades fall,
Mine was the guilt, and mine the sorrow, all;
How often have I sought thee —oft my mind
Figured thee to my sight —o'erjoyed to find
My mother's token; disappointment came,
When thou deniedst thy lineage and thy name;
Oh! still o'er thee my soul impassioned hung,
Still to my Father fond affection clung!
But Fate, remorseless, all my hopes withstood,
And stained thy reeking hands in kindred blood.'
    His faltering breath protracted speech denied
Still from his eyelids flowed a gushing tide;
Through Rostam's soul redoubled horror ran,
Heart-rending thoughts subdued the mighty man.
And now, at last, with joy-illumined eye,
The Zabol bands their glorious Chief descry;
But when they saw his pale and haggard look,
Knew from what mournful cause he gazed and shook,
With downcast mien they moaned and wept aloud;
While Rostam thus addressed the weeping crowd:
'Here ends the war! let gentle peace succeed,
Enough of death, I—I have done the deed!'
Then to his brother, groaning deep, he said:
'Oh what a curse upon a parent's head!
But go—and to the Tartar say—no more
Let war between us steep the earth with gore.'
Zuara flew and wildly spoke his grief
To crafty Houman, the Turanian Chief,
Who, with dissembled sorrow, heard him tell
The dismal tidings which he knew too well;
'And who,' he said, 'has caused these tears to flow?
Who but Hazhir? He might have stayed the blow;
But when Sohrab his Father's banners sought,
He still denied that here the Champion fought;

He spread the ruin, he the secret knew,
Hence should his crime receive the vengeance due!'
Zuara, frantic, breathed in Rostam's ear
The treachery of the captive Chief, Hazhir;
Whose headless trunk had weltered on the strand,
But prayers and force withheld the lifted hand.
Then to his dying son the Champion turned,
Remorse more deep within his bosom burned;
A burst of frenzy fired his throbbing brain;
He clenched his sword, but found his fury vain;
The Persian Chiefs the desperate act represt,
And tried to calm the tumult in his breast:
Thus Goudarz spoke: 'Alas! wert thou to give
Thyself a thousand wounds, and cease to live;
What would it be to him thou sorrowest o'er?
It would not save one pang—then weep no more;
For if removed by death, Oh say, to whom
Has ever been vouchsafed a different doom?
All are the prey of death—the crowned, the low,
And man, through life, the victim still of woe.'
Then Rostam : 'Fly! and to the King relate
The pressing horrors which involve my fate;
And if the memory of my deeds e'er swayed
His mind, Oh supplicate his generous aid;
A sovereign balm he has whose wondrous power
All wounds can heal, and fleeting life restore;
Swift from his tent the potent medicine bring.'
—But mark the malice of the brainless King!
Hard as the flinty rock, he stern denies
The healthful draught, and gloomy thus replies:
'Can I forgive his foul and slanderous tongue?
The sharp disdain on me contemptuous flung?
Scorned midst my army by a shameless boy,
Who sought my throne, my sceptre to destroy!
Nothing but mischief from his heart can flow:
Is it, then, wise to cherish such a foe?
The fool who warms his enemy to life,
Only prepares for scenes of future strife.'

Goudarz, returning, told the hopeless tale–
And thinking Rostam's presence might prevail,
The Champion rose, but ere he reached the throne,
Sohrab had breathed the last expiring groan.
Now keener anguish rack'd the father's mind,
Reft of his son, a murderer of his kind;
His guilty sword distained with filial gore,
He beat his burning breast, his hair he tore;
The breathless corse before his shuddering view,
A shower of ashes o'er his head he threw;
'In my old age,' he cried, 'what have I done?
Why have I slain my son, my innocent son!
Why o'er his splendid dawning did I roll
The clouds of death –and plunge my burthened soul
In agony? My son! from heroes sprung;
Better these hands were from my body wrung;
And solitude and darkness, deep and drear,
Fold me from sight than hated linger here.
But when his mother hears, with horror wild,
That I have shed the lifeblood of her child,
So nobly brave, so dearly loved, in vain,
How can her heart that rending shock sustain?'
Now on a bier the Persian warriors place
The breathless Youth, and shade his pallid face;
And turning from that fatal field away,
Move towards the Champion's home in long array.
Then Rostam, sick of martial pomp and show,
Himself the spring of all this scene of woe,
Doomed to the flames the pageantry he loved,
Shield, spear, and mace, so oft in battle proved;
Now lost to all, encompassed by despair;
His bright pavilion crackling blazed in air;
The sparkling throne the ascending column fed;
In smoking fragments fell the golden bed;
The raging fire red glimmering died away,
And all the Warrior's pride in dust and ashes lay.
Kavous, the King, now joins the mournful Chief,
And tries to soothe his deep and settled grief;

For soon or late we yield our vital breath,
And all our worldly troubles end in death!
'When first I saw him, graceful in his might,
He looked far other than a Tartar knight;
Wondering I gazed–now Destiny has thrown
Him on thy sword–he fought, and he is gone;
And should even Heaven against the earth be hurled,
Or fire inwrap in crackling flames the world,
That which is past-we never can restore,
His soul has travelled to some happier shore.
Alas! no good from sorrow canst thou reap,
Then wherefore thus in gloom and misery weep?'
But Rostam's mighty woes disdained his aid,
His heart was drowned in grief, and thus he said:
'Yes, he is gone! to me for ever lost!
Oh then protect his brave unguided host;
From war removed and this detested place,
Let them, unharmed, their mountain-wilds retrace;
Bid them secure my brother's will obey,
The careful guardian of their weary way,
To where the Jeihun's distant waters stray.'
To this the King: 'My soul is sad to see
Thy hopeless grief–but, since approved by thee,
The war shall cease–though the Turanian brand
Has spread dismay and terror through the land.'
The King, appeased, no more with vengeance burned,
The Tartar legions to their homes returned;
The Persian warriors, gathering round the dead,
Grovelled in dust, and tears of sorrow shed;
Then back to loved Iran their steps the monarch led.
But Rostam, midst his native bands, remained,
And further rites of sacrifice maintained;
A thousand horses bled at his command,
And the torn drums were scattered o'er the sand;
And now through Zabol's deep and bowery groves
In mournful pomp the sad procession moves.
The mighty Chief on foot precedes the bier;
His Warrior-friends in grief assembled near;

The dismal cadence rose upon the gale,
And Zal astonished heard the piercing wail;
He and his kindred joined the solemn train;
Hung round the bier and wondering viewed the slain.
'There gaze, and weep! the sorrowing Father said,
'For there, behold my glorious offspring dead!'
The hoary Sire shrunk backward with surprise,
And tears of blood o'erflowed his aged eyes;
And now the Champion's rural palace gate
Receives the funeral group in gloomy state;
Roudabeh loud bemoaned the Stripling's doom;
Sweet flower, all drooping in the hour of bloom,
His tender youth in distant bowers had past,
Sheltered at home he felt no withering blast;
In the soft prison of his mother's arms,
Secure from danger and the world's alarms.
Oh ruthless Fortune! flushed with generous pride,
He sought his sire, and thus unhappy, died.
  Rostam again the sacred bier unclosed;
Again Sohrab to public view exposed;
Husbands, and wives, and warriors, old and young,
Struck with amaze, around the body hung,
With garments rent and loosely flowing hair;
Their shrieks and clamours filled the echoing air;
Frequent they cried: 'Thus Sam the Champion slept!
Thus sleeps Sohrab!' Again they groaned, and wept.
  Now o'er the corpse a yellow robe is spread,
The aloes bier is closed upon the dead;
And, to preserve the hapless hero's name
Fragrant and fresh, that his unblemished fame
Might live and bloom through all succeeding days,
A mound sepulchral on the spot they raise,
Formed like a charger's hoof.
                                        In every ear
The story has been told—and many a tear
Shed at the sad recital. Through Turan,
Afrasiyab's wide realm, and Samengan,

Deep sunk the tidings —nuptial bower, and bed,
And all that promised happiness, had fled!
But when Tahmineh heard this tale of woe,
Think how a mother bore the mortal blow!
Distracted, wild, she sprang from place to place;
With frenzied hands deformed her beauteous face;
The musky locks her polished temples crowned,
Furious she tore, and flung upon the ground;
Starting, in agony of grief, she gazed—
Her swimming eyes to Heaven imploring raised;
And groaning cried: 'Sole comfort of my life!
Doomed the sad victim of unnatural strife,
Where art thou now with dust and blood defiled?
Thou darling boy, my lost, my murdered child!
When thou wert gone—how, night and lingering day,
Did thy fond mother watch the time away;
For hope still pictured all I wished to see,
Thy father found, and thou returned to me—
Yes, thou, exulting in thy father's fame!
And yet, nor sire nor son, nor tidings, came:
How could I dream of this? ye met —but how?
That noble aspect —that ingenuous brow,
Moved not a nerve in him —ye met —to part
Alas! the lifeblood issuing from the heart.
Short was the day which gave to me delight,
Soon, soon, succeeds a long and dismal night;
On whom shall now devolve my tender care?
Who, loved like thee, my bosom-sorrows share?
Whom shall I take to fill thy vacant place,
To whom extend a mother's soft embrace?
Sad fate! for one so young, so fair, so brave,
Seeking thy father thus to find a grave.
These arms no more shall fold thee to my breast,
No more with thee my soul be doubly blest;
No, drowned in blood thy lifeless body lies,
For ever torn from these desiring eyes;
Friendless, alone, beneath a foreign sky,
Thy mail thy death-clothes —and thy father by;

Why did I not conduct thee on the way,
And point where Rostam's bright pavilion lay?
Thou hadst the tokens –why didst thou withhold
Those dear remembrances –that pledge of gold?
Hadst thou the bracelet to his view restored,
Thy precious blood had never stained his sword.'
The strong emotion choked her panting breath,
Her veins seemed withered by the cold of death:
The trembling matrons hastening round her mourned,
With piercing cries, till fluttering life returned;
Then gazing up, distraught, she wept again,
And frantic, seeing midst her pitying train
The favourite steed –now more than ever dear,
The hoofs she kissed, and bathed with many a tear;
Clasping the mail Sohrab in battle wore,
With burning lips she kissed it o'er and o'er;
His martial robes she in her arms comprest,
And like an infant strained them to her breast;
The reins and trappings, club and spear, were brought,
The sword and shield with which the Stripling fought,
These she embraced with melancholy joy,
In sad remembrance of her darling boy.
And still she beat her face, and o'er them hung,
As in a trance, –or to them wildly clung–
Day after day she thus indulged her grief,
Night after night, disdaining all relief;
At length worn out –from earthly anguish riven,
The mother's spirit joined her child in Heaven.

J. Atkinson.

ROSTAM AND AKWAN DIV

KAI KHOSROW sat in a garden bright
With all the beauties of balmy spring;
And many a warrior, armour dight,
With a stout kamand and an arm of might,
Supported Persia's king.

With trembling mien and a pallid cheek,
A breathless hind to the presence ran,
And on bended knee in posture meek,
With faltering tongue that scarce could speak,
His story thus began:

'Alack-a-day! for the news I bear
Will like to the follies of fancy sound:
Thy steeds were stabled and stalled with care,
When a wild ass sprang from its forest lair,
With a swift resistless bound.

'A monster fell, of a dusky hue,
And eyes that flashed with a hellish glow,
Many it maimed and some it slew,
Then back to the forest again it flew,
As an arrow leaves the bow.'

Kaikhosrow's rage was a sight to see;
'Now curses light on the foul fiend's head!
Full rich and rare shall his guerdon be
Whose stalwart arm shall bring to me
The monster, live or dead.'

But the mail-clad warriors kept their ground.
And their bronzed cheeks were blanched with fear.
With scorn the Shah on the cowards frowned:
'One champion bold may yet be found
While Rostam wields a spear!'

No tarrying made the son of Zal,
Small reck had he of the fiercest fray,
But promptly came at the monarch's call,
And swore that the monster fiend should fall,
Ere closed the coming day.

The swift Rakhsh's sides he spurred,
And speedily gained the darksome wood;
Nor was the trial for long deferred,
But soon a hideous roar was heard,
Had chilled a baser blood.

Then darting out like a flashing flame,
Traverse his path the wild ass fled;
And the hero then with unerring aim
Hurled his stout kamand, but as erst it came,
Unscathed the monster fled.

'Now Khoda in Heaven,' bold Rostam cried,
'Thy chosen champion deign to save!
Not all in vain shall my steel be tried,
Though he who my powers has thus defied
Were none but Akwan Div.'

Then steadily chasing his fiendish foe,
He thrust with hanger, and smote with brand;
But ever avoiding the deadly blow,
It vanished away like the scenes that show
On Balkh's delusive sand.

For full three wearisome nights and days
Stoutly he battled with warlike skill;
But the demon such magical shifts assays,
That leaving his courser at large to graze,
He rests him on a hill.

But scarce cart slumber his eyelids close,
Ere Akwan Div from afar espies;
And never disturbing his foe's repose,
The earth from under the mound he throws,
And off with the summit flies.

'Now, daring mortal,' the demon cried,
'Whither wouldst have me carry thee?
Shall I cast thee forth on the mountain side,
Where the lions roar and the reptiles glide,
Or hurl thee into the sea?'

'Oh, bear me off to the mountain side,
Where the lions roar and the serpents creep;
For I fear not the creatures that spring or glide,
But where is the arm that can stem the tide,
Or still the raging deep?'

Loud laughed the fiend as his load he threw,
Far plunging into the roaring flood;
And louder laughed Rostam as out he flew,
For he fain had chosen the sea, but knew
The fiend's malignant mood.

Soon all the monsters that float or swim,
With ravening jaws down on him bore;
But he hewed and he hacked them limb from limb,
And the wave pellucid grew thick and dim
With streaks of crimson gore.

With thankful bosom he gains the strand,
And seeketh his courser near and far,
Till he hears him neigh and he sees him stand
Among the herds of a Tartar band,
The steeds of Isfandiar.

But Rostam's name was a sound of dread,
And the Tartar heart it had caused to quake;
The herd was there, but the hinds had fled,
So all the horses he captive led
For good Kaikhosrow's sake.

Then loud again through the forest rings
The fiendish laugh and the taunting cry;
But his kamand quickly the hero flings,
And around the demon it coils and clings,
As a cobweb wraps a fly.

Kaikhosrow sat in his garden fair,
Mourning his champion lost and dead,
When a shout of victory rent the air,
And Rostam placed before his chair
A demon giant's head!

E. H. Palmer.

A horsewoman with a pigeon in hand, Naser Oweisi, 78×99 cm., 1950s

A polo player, Naser Oweisi, 114×132 cm., 1963

INDEX OF POETS

HAFEZ (1320-91) of Shiraz, the greatest lyric poet of Persia, has attracted very many translators. page 60

EQBAL (1876-1938) of Lahore, eminent lawyer, philosopher, and statesman, a founder of Pakistan, wrote many lyrics and didactic poems in Persian and Urdu. He was an advocate of religious reform in Islam. page 136

IRAJ (d. 1925) was regarded as one of the leading poets of his generation, marking the transition from classical to modem style. page 85

IRAQI (d. 1289), mystic, composed many odes, a religious didactic poem, and a short treatise in verse and prose on divine love. page 57

JAMI (817-92), commonly called the last great classical poet of Persia, saint and mystic, composed numerous lyrics and idylls, as well as many works in prose. His *Salaman and Absal* is a fine allegory of profane and sacred love. pages 81, 171

KHANLARI (contemporary) is a leading poet and critic of the younger generation. pages 89, 141

NASER KHOSROW (1003-61), traveller, Isma'ili missionary, wrote many odes of a religious and moralizing character, as well as prose works describing his travels and making propaganda for the sectarian views he adopted. . page 99

NEZAMI (1140-1202) of Ganja, the greatest writer of idyll, composed five long poems on various themes, including the desert romance of Kais (Majnun, the Madman) and Laili. Manuscripts of his poems are adorned with splendid miniatures. page 149

OMAR KHAYYAM (d. 1123 or 1132), mathematician astronomer, and philosopher, is the greatest composer of *ruba'iyat* or quatrains. Since FitzGerald's brilliant paraphrase he has been translated into all the major languages of the world. pages 3, 16

PARVIN (d. 1941), the greatest poetess in Persian literature, died at an early age after writing much, chiefly in the didactic vein, which earned her a wide reputation. page 140

RUDAKI (d. 940), the first major poet of Islamic Persia, a fertile writer of whose stupendous output comparatively little has survived, is chiefly esteemed for his odes. page 93

RUMI (1207-73), saint and mystic, founder of the Molavi order of whirling dervishes, who was born at Balkh and died at Konia (Turkey), wrote many odes and quatrains, and is chiefly famous for his great didactic epic of the religious life. pages 33, 46, 118

SA'DI (1184?-1292) of Shiraz, greatest didactic poet of Persia, author of the *Gulistan* ('Rose-Garden') and *Bustan* ('Orchard'), also wrote many fine odes and lyrics. pages51, 128

SANA'I (*fl.* 1150) composed numerous odes and lyrics and a religious epic. He is reckoned the first of the great mystical poets of Persia. pages 41, 117

SHAHRIYAR (contemporary) writes lyrics in the modern fashion. page 107

TAVALLALI (contemporary) is an imagist poet. page 86

YASIMI (contemporary) writes chiefly in the didactic style. page 140

INDEX OF TRANSLATORS

ARTHUR JOHN ARBERRY, born in 1905 at Portsmouth, was educated at Portsmouth Grammar School and Pembroke College, Cambridge, where he read classics and oriental languages. After spending three years in Egypt, he was a civil servant from 1934 to 1944. During the 1939-45 war he worked in the Postal Censorship (Uncommon Languages Department) and the Ministry of Information. In 1944 he was elected Professor of Persian in the University of London, in 1946 Professor of Arabic there, and in 1947 Professor of Arabic at Cambridge. He is a Fellow of Pembroke College, a Fellow of the British Academy, and a Corresponding Member of the Egyptian, Syrian, and Persian Academies. (Pages 33-7, 42-6, 49-50, 53-7, 58-9, 77-80, 82-9, 106-13, 136-46.)

SIR EDWIN ARNOLD (1832-1904), born at Gravesend and educated at King's School, Rochester, King's College, London, and University College, Oxford, obtained a third in classics, and in 1852 won the Newdigate Prize. After teaching for a short time at King Edward's School, Birmingham, in 1856 he went out to India as Principal of Deccan College, Poona. Five years later he answered an advertisement and was appointed a leader-writer on the Daily Telegraph, of which he was later a chief editor. He was knighted in 1888, and was a brother of Sir Arthur Arnold (1833-1902), the radical politician. He wrote very many books on a great variety of subjects, and much poetry, his most celebrated poem being *The Light of Asia* (1879). (Pages 135-6.)

JAMES ATKINSON (1780-1852) was born in Co. Durham, and studied medicine at Edinburgh and London. His first appointment was as medical officer on board an East Indiaman. This led to his becoming a surgeon in Bengal. From 1813 to 1828 he was assistant assay master at the Calcutta Mint; in 1818 he was deputy professor of Persian at Fort William College; from 1817 to 1828 he was superintendent of the *Government Gazette*. He spent the years 1828-33 in England returning to India as surgeon to the 55th regiment of Indian infantry; he rose to become a member of the Medical Board in 1845, retired in 1847, and died of apoplexy. In addition to his translations of Ferdowsi and Nezami, he wrote books on

Afghanistan, volumes of original verse, and translations from the Italian; and, in 1831, 'A Description of the New Process of Perforating and Destroying the Stone in the Bladder.' (Pages 149-60, 196-219.)

GERTRUDE MARGARET LOWTHIAN BELL (1868-1926) was born in Co. Durham, daughter of Sir Thomas Bell, ironmaster. She was educated at Queen's College, Harley Street and Lady Margaret Hall, Oxford, where in 1888 she graduated with a first in modern history. She almost immediately began her extensive travels, visiting Persia for the first time in 1892-3; her impressions are described in *Persian Sketches* (1894), and her translations from Hafez belong to this period. She was an enthusiastic and skilful mountaineer, her most remarkable feat being an ascent of the Matterhorn from the Italian side. Her later visits to Syria, Turkey, and Mesopotamia were associated with archaeological exploration, commemorated in her *Amurath to Amurath* (1911). In 1913-14 she penetrated Arabia proper, and in the 1914-18 war she was a member of the celebrated Arab Bureau. When Bagdad fell she was appointed oriental secretary, first to Sir Percy Cox and later to Sir Arnold Wilson. In 1918 she became the first Director of Antiquities of Iraq, and laboured to build the National Museum. She died quite suddenly in her sleep. Her *Letters* were published posthumously and are much admired.

(Pages 67-71.)

EDWARD GRANVILLE BROWNE (1862-1926), born at Uley in Gloucestershire, son of Sir Benjamin Browne, a civil engineer, was educated at Eton and Pembroke College, Cambridge. He took the Natural Science Tripos in 1882 and the Indian Languages Tripos in 1884; originally intended for medicine, he attained the M.B. in 1887 but never practised. In the same year he was elected to a fellowship and visited Persia, returning to a lectureship in Persian at Cambridge; in 1902 he was appointed to Sir Thomas Adams's Professorship in Arabic, and became a Fellow of the British Academy the following year. In 1911 the F.R.C.P. was conferred upon him. His most famous work is his four-volume *Literary History of Persia*, but he edited and wrote much besides, being particularly interested in the Babi movement and in democratic reform in Persia. His death was marked in Persia as a public day of mourning. (Pages 41, 51, 57, 95-101, 117-18.)

JOSEPH CHAMPION, servant of the Honourable East India Company, was appointed a writer on the Bengal establishment in 1778. In 1779 he was paymaster to the Cavalry Brigade; nine years later he was a Junior Merchant, by which time he had published his translations from Ferdowsi. In 1791 he was sent home to Europe suffering from mental derangement. (Pages 183-96.)

GEORGE SCOTT DAVIE (1835-96) joined the Army Medical Service in 1858 as an assistant surgeon; his promotion to surgeon, and then surgeon major, came in 1873. After serving in Perak, the Afghan War of 1878-9, and Egypt during the Orabi Pasha rebellion of 1882, he was gazetted brigade surgeon in 1885, and retired the following year with the honorary rank of deputy surgeon general. His volume of translations from Sa'di appears to have been his only adventure in Persian studies. (Pages 133-5.)

EDWARD BACKHOUSE EASTWICK (1814-83), educated at Charterhouse and Merton College, Oxford, went out to India in 1836 as a cadet in the Bombay infantry. His special gifts led to an early transfer to the civil administration, but his health broke down and he returned to England. In 1845 he was appointed Professor of Hindustani at the East India Company's college at Haileybury. In 1860 he was called to the Middle Temple, and in the same year went to Tehran as secretary of legation, a post he held for three years. Lord Cranborne (the Marquis of Salisbury), as Secretary of State for India in 1866, appointed him his private secretary. From 1868 to 1874 he represented Penryn and Falmouth in Parliament. He wrote many books on Persian and Hindustani, and composed a series of manuals on India and the Indian provinces. (Page 130.)

EDWARD FITZGERALD (1809-83) was born at Woodbridge, Suffolk, and was educated at Bury St Edmunds and Trinity College, Cambridge, where he was a contemporary of the three Tennyson brothers. He lived in retirement in Suffolk, and had many distinguished friends in the literary world, prominent among them Tennyson and Carlyle. In 1853 he published a translation of six dramas of Carlyle. He took up the study of Persian at the instance of Professor E. B. Cowell, and in 1856 produced his *Salaman and Absal*. The first edition of his paraphrase of Omar Khayyam came out three years later, and was at first a failure. His

Bird-Parliament was not published until after his death. (Pages 3-32, 160-79.)

JOHN HADDON HINDLEY (1765-1827), son of Charles Hindley, a mercer, was educated at Manchester Grammar School and Brasenose College, Oxford. After graduation he was appointed chaplain of Manchester Collegiate Church, and was put in charge of Chetham Library. It was there that he took up the study of Persian. Being a man described as 'reserved and crotchety,' he lost his reason in later life and died at Clapham. (Pages59-60, 65-6.)

ABRAHAM VALENTINE WILLIAMS JACKSON (1862-1937) was born in New York, and pursued his higher studies at Columbia University and Halle. From 1891 to 1895 he was adjoint-professor of English at Columbia, after which he occupied the Chair of Indo-Iranian Languages to his retirement in 1935. He travelled widely in Asia, and wrote much on Zoroastrianism and Avestan studies. He was president of the Omar Khayyam Society of America from 1927 to 1929. (Pages 93-4.)

SIR WILLIAM JONES (1746-94) was born in London, son of William Jones, F.R.S. He was educated at Harrow and University College, Oxford, and early displayed a remarkable gift for languages. In 1766 he became private tutor to Lord Althorp, the son and heir of Earl Spencer. In 1770 he was admitted to the Temple, and was called to the Bar in 1774, by which time he had published his Persian grammar and his volume of poetry, and been admitted a member of The Club of Samuel Johnson. After practising law successfully for some years, and playing a part in Whig politics, in 1783 he was appointed a judge in the High Court of Calcutta. He passed the rest of his short life in India, where he was extremely influential in stimulating oriental studies; he founded the Asiatic Society, wrote and published much on a wide variety of subjects, and encouraged others to write and publish. His collected works were published posthumously, with a biography by Lord Teignmouth. His portrait by Sir Joshua Reynolds is in the possession of Earl Spencer. (Pages 60-2, 81, 118-19, 128.)

THOMAS LAW (1759-1834), seventh son of Edmund Law, Bishop of Carlisle, went out to India in the Company's service in 1773, and after serving brilliantly in the revenue department he returned sick to England in 1791. Two years later he emigrated to the United States; he married a grand-daughter of George Washington, and attended the great president's funeral as one of the chief mourners. Though he laboured capably and successfully to establish the national currency of the new republic, his own financial operations were less fortunate and he died in comparative poverty. (Pages 63-4.)

WALTER LEAF (1852-1927), son of Charles John Leaf, silk and ribbon dealer, was educated at Harrow, where Dean Farrar made him head of his house. Elected a classical scholar by Trinity College, Cambridge, he was bracketed Senior Classic in 1874 and became a fellow the next year. However, his father falling sick he felt himself obliged to resign academic work and enter the family business. Later he turned to banking, and in 1918 became chairman of the London and Westminster Bank. Throughout his busy life he never deserted his original love, and attained high distinction as a Homeric scholar. He was a gifted linguist, and Persian was but one of many learned diversions. Pages 71-2.)

RICHARD LE GALLIENNE (1866-1947), born at Liverpool, was educated at Liverpool College. Having served his articles with a firm of chartered accountants, he turned to literary work and became critic to the *Star*. He published many volumes of essays, poems, and literary studies, and made a version of Omar Khayyam as well as of Hafez. (Pages 74-6.)

WALTER CARR MACKINNON, born in 1834, made his career in the army in India, rising from ensign in 1852 to colonel in 1889, in which year he retired. (Pages 131-3.)

REYNOLD ALLEYNE NICHOLSON (1868-1945), son of Henry Alleyne Nicholson, F.R.S., was educated at Edinburgh, Aberdeen, and Trinity College, Cambridge, where he read for the Classical Tripos and the Indian Languages Tripos, being elected to a fellowship in 1893. In 1901 he was appointed Professor of Persian at University College, London, but two years later returned to Cambridge as lecturer in Persian. He succeeded E. G. Browne in 1926 as Sir Thomas Adams's Professor of Arabic, and retired in 1933. He was a most prolific author, editor, and translator, specializing in literature and mysticism.

His best-known works are his *Literary History of the Arabs* and his great edition and translation of Rumi. (Pages 46-8, 52, 76-7, 125-8.)

JOHN NOTT (1751-1825) was born at Worcester, his father, of German descent, being a favourite retainer of George III. Having studied surgery at Birmingham and London, in 1783 he went out to China as surgeon in an East Indiaman, and learned Persian on his tour of duty. He returned to practice medicine in England, settling at Hot Wells, Bristol. He wrote copiously on literature and medicine, translating Petrarch, Propertius, Catullus, Lucretius, and Horace. His somewhat pedantic annotations on George Wither attracted abusive comment from Charles Lamb and Swinburne. (Pages 64-5.)

EDWARD HENRY PALMER (1840-82), born at Cambridge, was educated at Perse School; he left at 16 to join a City firm of wine merchants. A natural linguist, he picked up Romany from gipsies and Italian and French from dockside acquaintances; he also discovered himself possessed of remarkable mesmeric powers, and early formed a firm friendship with Henry Irving. In 1859 he developed consumption and returned to Cambridge apparently dying, but made an astonishing recovery. He now took up oriental languages; his aptitude being recognized by St John's College, he was awarded a sizarship and took a third in the Classical Tripos in 1867, was nevertheless elected to a fellowship, and forthwith travelled in Sinai and Palestine. In 1871 he was appointed Lord Almoner's Professor of Arabic. Ten years later he added journalism to his teaching duties, having already published many books. In 1882 he was sent to Egypt on a secret mission by the Foreign Office, there to be murdered by Bedouin marauders. He was buried in the crypt of St Paul's. (Pages 66-7, 101-6, 120-4, 219-23.)

JOHN PAYNE (1842-1916), born in Bloomsbury, at the age of 13 moved with his parents to Bristol. He passed his early years as a clerk and an usher, but before reaching 19 he had made verse translations of Dante, Goethe, Calderon, and Lessing. He was an amazing self-taught linguist, and his numerous publications, many privately printed, include translations of the Arabian Nights, Villon, Omar Khayyam, Boccaccio, Bandello, and Heine; he also wrote several volumes of original poetry.

He was a hotly controversial figure, his admirers praising him extravagantly; for all that he is not noticed in the Dictionary of National Biography. His style exhibits the extreme tendencies of Victorian neo-Gothic. (Pages 72-4.)

EBENEZER POCOCK, who made a metrical version of the *Book of Advice* of Sa'di, appears not to have written anything else, and this must be his only adventure in literature. (Pages 129-30.)

SIR JAMES WILLIAM REDHOUSE (1811-92), born near London and educated at Christ's Hospital, was employed by the Ottoman Government as a draughtsman in 1826. Four years later he went to Russia, but in 1838 he was re-employed by the Sublime Porte, and in 1840 he was attached to the Turkish admiralty. Thereafter he served as an intermediary between Turkey and Great Britain, until in 1854 he was appointed oriental translator at the Foreign Office. Cambridge conferred on him the honorary doctorate of letters in 1884, and in 1888 he was made K.C.M.G. He published many books, especially on Turkish language and literature. (Pages 124-5.)

JOHN RICHARDSON (1741-1811?), born at Edinburgh, was educated at Wadham College, Oxford, and entered the Middle Temple in 1781. He gave Sir William Jones some assistance with his grammar of Persian; his chief work was his Persian dictionary, first issued in two volumes in 1777. Pages 62-3.)

SIR EDWARD DENISON ROSS (1871-1940) was born in Stepney, and was educated at University College, London and in Paris. In 1896 he was appointed Professor of Persian at University College; five years later he went out to India as principal of Calcutta Madrasa, where he served for ten years. After a brief employment in the British Museum, in 1916 he was chosen as the first Director of the London School of Oriental Languages. Early in the 1939-45 war he was sent to Turkey on patriotic duties; there he died and is buried. He was knighted in 1918. A versatile linguist, he published many books on a wide range of oriental studies. (Page 58.)

STEPHEN WESTON (1747-1830), born at Exeter, a grandson of Stephen Weston, Bishop of Exeter, was educated at Blundell's School and Exeter College, Oxford, where he was Devonshire Fellow from 1768 to 1784. He was rector of Little Hempston from 1784 to 1823, was elected Fellow of the Royal Society in 1792, and Fellow of the Society of Antiquaries in 1794. A dilettante in the best sense of the word, he published on a wide variety of topics, frolicking with Chinese, Sanskrit, and Arabic as well as Persian. His portrait by Sir Joshua Reynolds hangs in Exeter College hall. (Pages 82, 128.)

GLOSSARY

abdals: great saints, seventy in number, who are thought to preside over the destinies of the world.
Absal: the nurse of Salaman in Jami's idyll Salaman and Absal, typifying profane love.
Afrasiyab: ancient king of Turin (Turkestan).
Afridun: ancient king of Persia.
Ahmad: another name for the Prophet Mohammad.
Akwan Div: a powerful demon, destroyed by Rostam.
Alif: the first letter of the Arabic alphabet, symbolizing (on account of its shape) a tall and erect stature.
Am'ak: court poet of Bukhara, died A.D. 1148.
amir: prince or commander.
Arafa: mountain near Mecca, visited by the faithful during the pilgrimage.
Asaf: King Solomon's chief minister.
Ashura: the anniversary of the death of Hosain, son of Ali, the 9th or 10th day of the month of Muharram.
Badakhshan: a region in Central Asia famous for its rubies.
Bahram: ancient king of Persia (Bahram Gur), famous for his addiction to hunting the wild ass.
Belqais: the Queen of Saba.
bulbul: the Persian nightingale.
dinar: gold coin.
dirham: silver coin.
Eram: fabled gardens of ancient Arabia.
'Eid:: festival.
Farhad: lover of the Princess Shirin, who dug through a huge mountain to attain his beloved.
farman: royal edict.
ferrash: chamberlain, executioner.
First Chapter: the Fatiha; the opening Sura of the Koran.
gav: the bull, Taurus, the legendary creature on whose horns the earth is supposed to rest.
harim: harem.
Hatam: ancient Arab famed for his generosity.
Houshang: ancient Persian king, second of the Pishdadi dynasty.
Isfandiar, Isfendiyar: son of Goshtasp, ancient Persian king.
Jam: ancient king of Persia.
Jamshid: ancient Persian king, possessor of a magic cup in which he could see the whole world mirrored.

Ka'ba: the sanctuary of Mecca containing the famous Black Stone.
Kafer: unbeliever.
Kai: royal title, great king.
Kaikhosrow: Cyrus, a great king.
Kaiqobad: ancient Persian king.
Qaf: mountain range supposed to encircle the earth.
Qais: old Arab poet, lover of Laili, called Majnun (Madman).
kamand: noose, halter.
Kavous: ancient king of Persia.
Khata: Cathay.
Khezr: mysterious saint or prophet, chief minister to Alexander the Great, who discovered the Water of Life.
Khosrow: royal title, ancient Persian king.
Khoda: God.
King's arrow: arrow granting immunity.
Kiyumars: first of the Pishdadi kings of Persia.
Kosrow: Chosroes, royal title.
Kouzehnameh: 'Book of the Pitcher,' title given by FitzGerald to a sequence of quatrains from Omar Khayyam.
Laili: beloved of Qais.
mah: the moon.
mahi: the legendary fish on which the earth is said to rest.
Mahmoud: famous king of Ghazna, conqueror of India.
Majnun: nickname given to Qais, the poet-lover of Laili.
Manuchehr: ancient Persian king.
Mosalla, Mosellay: celebrated gardens of Shiraz.
Moses, white hand of: a miracle recorded in the Koran.
muezzin: the functionary who calls the faithful to prayer.
Museilima: false prophet defeated by the early Moslem *champion Khaled.*
Mushtari: the planet Jupiter.
nergiss: the narcissus.
Night of Merit: the 27th of Ramazan, when the Koran is said to have descended from heaven and powerful spirits walk abroad.
Nijid: Nejd, mountainous region of Arabia.
Nirum: Nariman, father of Sam.
Pahlavi: the pre-Islamic language of Persia.
Parwin: the Pleiades.
Pen, the Eternal: the Heavenly Pen.
Peri: fairy.
Rakhsh: name of Rustam's famous horse.
Ramazan: month of the Moslem fast.
Roknabad: famous stream of Shiraz.
Room, Rum: Byzantium, Turkey.

Rostam: son of Zal, celebrated Persian hero.
saki: wine-bearer, sometimes symbolizing the creative spirit of God.
Salaman: hero of Jami's *Salaman and Absal*, symbolizing the human soul questing reunion with God.
Salsabil: river of Paradise.
Sam: grandfather of Rostam.
Saman: founder of the Samanid dynasty of Persian kings.
Sanjar: celebrated Seljuk monarch.
Sham: Syria.
Shirin: beautiful Persian princess, beloved by Farhad.
Siamak: son of King Kiyumars.
Simorgh: the fabulous griffin in Attar's *Bird-Parliament* symbolizing the Spirit of God; in Ferdowsi's *Shahnameh* the foster-father and teacher of Zal.*Sohrab*: son of Rostam.
Solaiman: Solomon.
Sufi: Mohammedan mystic.
Tabriz's Sun: Shams-e Tabriz, the teacher of Rumi.
Tahmineh: the mother of Sohrab.
Tajidar: the phoenix.
Turan: Turkestan.
Water of Life: fabulous fountain conferring immortality.
Yusof: Joseph.
Zal: father of Rostam.
Zohreh: the planet Venus.

